What Others are Sayi[ng about]
Soul Care When You're [Grieving]

We all have two hemispheres in our brains. The left is largely logical, and the right is artistic, emotional, and creative. Some of us try to left-brain our way through grief with miserable results. Grief refuses to be confined to logic; in reality, the extreme emotions caused by loss can prove too difficult to describe with the limited vocabulary of our left brain. Edie Melson understands the importance of engaging the right brain's language of imagery and creativity to process grief. With sensitivity and honesty, she guides the brokenhearted on a journey of healing, one prayer and creative practice at a time. Even the most logical among us will be astonished at the power of art to access and release the complex feelings grief imposes on the soul.

~Audrey Frank, Group Facilitator, The Trauma Healing Institute, author of *Covered Glory: The Face of Honor and Shame in the Muslim World* (Harvest House Publishers, 2019).

In this exquisitely written book, Edie Melson, a fellow sojourner, speaks heart to heart with those who grieve. As a survivor of personal tragedies, and horrific life altering losses, Melson shares her raw, honest reactions, deep soul-searching questions and a myriad of pathways back to a feeling of closeness to the Great Healer who never let her go. As a psychotherapist who loves bibliotherapy, so many times I wished for a book like *Soul Care When You're Grieving*. Each section is balm for a burn, identifying the issues, addressing the mind traps, guiding without preaching, and offering suggestions of what to "do" with the turmoil. When someone experiences grief, I will never again wonder, "how can I help?" With great confidence, I will give them this book.

~Deborah McCormick Maxey PhD Licensed Professional Counselor, Licensed Marriage and Family Therapist, Certified Traumatologist

As a former hospital chaplain, I witnessed grief on a daily basis. In the last year, I've watched my friend, Edie Melson, experience the searing pain that comes with the loss of a loved one and the grief that accompanies it. She knows firsthand the long and lonely road of grief she describes in her new book. The ancient Greek author, Aeschylus, famously observed: "Even in our sleep, pain which cannot forget falls drop by drop upon the heart until, in our own despair, against our will, comes wisdom through the awful grace of God." In this life, we will all experience grief - the price we pay for loving others. But not everyone allows that process to bring forth the wisdom that Aeschylus describes. In *Soul Care When You're Grieving*, Edie shares precious nuggets of the wisdom she has already mined in her grief journey with the hope that you, the reader, will allow your pain to eventually be transformed into wisdom as well.

~Dr. Craig von Buseck, Author and Managing Editor at Inspiration.org

Soul Care When You're Grieving by author Edie Melson is a hope-filled gift to anyone walking the hard path of grief. Melson understands because she's learned to carry the weight of grief, rather than letting it overwhelm her. Melson shares honestly about her struggles, helping others know they are not alone. By utilizing her prayers, readers can begin to form their own. By working through the various exercises, readers can creatively explore their thoughts and emotions and move forward to healing.

~Beth K. Vogt
Christy Award & Carol Award Winner

I finished reading *Soul Care When You're Grieving* hours before my son was killed in a tragic accident. The words and compassion that filled each sentence now filled my heart.

Through her own experiences, Edie Melson guides the reader from loss to healing with spiritual truths and creative art forms. Highly recommended.

Soul Care When You're Grieving uses biblical truths and creative art forms to work through loss and move closer to healing.

Soul Care When You're Grieving provides spiritual insight through journaling, creativity, and various art forms to heal from loss.

~DiAnn Mills, Christy Award Winner

Edie Melson has written a book no one wants to read—but everyone needs to read. Eventually, we all suffer loss—a job, a relationship, a loved one. When we do (or because we have), we need the poignant comfort *Soul Care When You're Grieving* provides. Like a kind friend, Edie walks the broken path beside us—sometimes cheering us on, other times weeping with us. With wisdom and insight gained from her own unimaginable losses, Edie has been divinely equipped to show us the way through the darkness and into the light.

~Lori Hatcher, Author of *Refresh Your Faith,*
Uncommon Devotions from
Every Book of the Bible

With a gentle hand and warm embrace, Edie Melson, comes alongside you in your pain, holding you up and leading you out to places you never thought possible. If you find yourself stuck in sorrow, *Soul Care When You're Grieving* opens the door to explore those overwhelming emotions and finds hope again. This book is the perfect gift to give to someone who is grieving and also to have on your shelf, ready to offer when the unthinkable happens.

~Erica Wiggenhorn– Bible teacher and author of
Letting God Be Enough: Why Striving Keeps You Stuck
and *How Surrender Sets You Free*

When we grieve, there's a chance we can lose our creative spirit to a spirit of hurt, hate, and heartbreak. Edie Melson's weekly invitations to engage with God's word in a compassionate way, as she transparently shares her story, not only preserves our creativity but ignites in us the ability to consider a life of more, beyond our loss. How beautiful it is to pick up a guide that doesn't tell us what to do with our grief but simply walks hand-in-hand with us as we go.

~Linda Goldfarb, International Speaker, Award-winning Author, Advanced Certified Life Coach, LivePowerfullyNow.org

Author Edie Melson never asked for credentials as an expert on grief through first-hand experience—life just happened. Yet, because of her diligence in seeking redemption from her own losses, we the readers of *Soul Care When You're Grieving* are both comforted and challenged by her exquisite words. The authenticity and vulnerability revealed in each prayer is a balm (anyone who has turned away help will resonate with "A Prayer Asking for the Presence of God's People.") Perhaps what sets this book apart is the interactive creativity that ministers to our souls as we are processing the grief journey. Though I'm not particularly crafty, I have discovered that coloring, photography, doodling, music, and even stickers can be a portal into the unknown I'm seeking to understand and embrace – they give me something to do whilst pointing me to God, nature, hope, and a new normal. This book would be a helpful companion for anyone faced with loss, and sadly, that is most of us today.

~Lucinda Secrest McDowell, award-winning author of *"Soul Strong"* **and** *"Life-Giving Choices"*

Soul Care
When You're Grieving

Soul Care When You're Grieving

Edie Melson

Bold Vision Books
PO Box 2011
Friendswood, Texas 77549

Dedication

This book is lovingly dedicated to
my precious daughter-in-law Katie Melson,
and all those whose lives are
sweeter because you are
forever part of us.

Table of Contents

Acknowledgments

No book can see the light of day without an entire team of people moving it forward. That's especially true of this book. When I first envisioned it, I did not know tragedy would befall our family. But it's this family—and our wider faith family who fueled the diligence to finish putting words to page. So, a huge thank you goes first to my family. Kirklyn Melson, my precious and encouraging husband. I also want to thank my kids, Jimmy, Kirk, Weslyn, John, and Tiffany. Finally, I couldn't have continued without the support of my amazing sister, Katy, and my mother.

I also want to thank those who have given this project much needed—daily—prayer support. You are just too numerous to name. I also want to thank my Friday morning, More Than Sunday, accountability group. You guys are an inspiration.

And I could never leave out my critique group with Lynette Eason, Molly Jo Realy, Tammy Karasek, Alycia Morales, Lynn Blackburn, Linda Gilden, Erynn Newman, Emme Gannon, Michelle Cox, Tim Suddeth and Larry Leech. A special shout out goes to my ever-patient agent, Blythe Daniel. Of course, I want to include everyone at Bold Vision Books. You are the greatest group any author could ever hope to be blessed with.

No writer can ever move ahead without other writers to share the journey! A special thank you goes to my sister-friend, DiAnn Mills and to my prayer partner, encourager extraordinaire, Beth Vogt. I love doing life with you all.

Introduction

Grief is difficult. We all experience it—and we experience it differently. There is no right or wrong way to face loss, yet many of us feel we're doing it wrong.

In this life, we mourn—the loss of someone we love, the passing of a pet, the changes that come with age, even situations—these cause us to grieve. I wrote this book about the grief of all those situations and more. The exercises contained here aren't geared to a specific situation, so they are appropriate for all kinds of loss.

Going through loss narrows my world. I used to believe that was my personal experience, but I've discovered it's a common grief that happens to us all. I'm praying this book helps you break down the barriers created by grief and helps you engage with the world around you.

Most of all, I pray you learn to embrace your own process of grief and quit judging whether you're handling things the way they should be handled. God designed each of us uniquely, and that blueprint includes the way we process loss.

Each chapter is designated by the *opposite* of one of the five experiences of grief. It's far too easy to be tied to the common misconceptions about grief, so by reframing them, I'm hoping you'll give yourself more grace as you process your loss.

These stages of grief are not steps or levels, they are just some common phases everyone goes through while they process loss. Don't fall into the trap of believing they come in a certain order or that when you've experienced one of them, it won't crop back up again.

Use this book to feed your soul when you're grieving and know my prayer team and I have prayed over your personal journey. Remember, you are not alone in your grief. God is always with you—whether or not you're aware of Him.

Optional Supply List

My desire is for this book to be something you use. My prayer is that it will be become dog-eared and stained from carrying it around. I urge you to draw in it, experiment, and learn once again the healing power of play—especially play with our Heavenly Father.

You can use this book with nothing more than a pen or pencil. But if you want to go further, here is a list of supplies you might enjoy using:

- [ ] Colored pencils
- [ ] Markers, fine tip, brush, and/or glitter
- [ ] Paint, acrylic and/or watercolor
- [ ] Washi tape
- [ ] Stickers
- [ ] Gelato sticks
- [ ] Journal
- [ ] Glue
- [ ] Glitter
- [ ] Ribbon

In addition, there are several instances where I encourage you to take a photograph. You don't need special equipment.

- [ ] Cell phone camera
- [ ] An Instamatic of some kind, like Fujifilm
- [ ] Instax or Polaroid Snap
- [ ] Digital camera

Chapter One

Moving Past Denial

Denial is where most of us begin our journey through grief. Initially, we refuse to believe the worst has indeed happened. More than that, we struggle with constant reminders of the one we've lost who should be present with us.

Our daughter-in-law's tragic accident and death rocked my world. She left my son with a three-month-old infant, and the unfairness of losing a young mother brought on questions and anger that were difficult beyond imagining.

When I lost my best friend suddenly, everywhere I looked I glimpsed her. From behind, so many strangers looked like Jennifer. Each time I chased down that hope, the person I saw was not my friend, and the grief was once again new, raw, and almost unbearable.

Losing my father to Alzheimer's was different. Much of the grieving took place during his illness. Yet there were still times after his passing when a piece of music or an unexpected image would bring him to mind. During those instances, I argued with myself about the fact that he was gone.

I based this denial on my struggle to give myself permission to move forward without my dear one. There were so many reasons I didn't want to move on. Most of all, moving forward felt like a betrayal—as if I was forgetting their importance in my life. By constantly denying the fact they were gone, I kept the memories alive—or so I told myself. All I was keeping alive was the pain of their passing.

That pain also blocked the joyful moments of their living. By focusing on the pain, I denied myself the beauty of remembering the good parts of life with them.

But losing a person isn't the only reason we face seasons of grief. The year 2020 and its resulting pandemic pushed thousands into grief as they lost homes, jobs, loved ones, and a way of life that can never be recaptured. That grief can be just as traumatic. Sometimes grieving circumstances can be even more life altering. With a situational change, we don't always feel we have permission to feel that intensity of pain and emotions. We have that permission. And it's only when we acknowledge and process the emotions that we can move on in life.

Through the devotions, creative moments, and prayers, we'll travel through this process of giving ourselves permission to move forward.

God's Strength is Enough

And He has said to me, "My grace is sufficient for
you, for power is perfected in weakness.
"Most gladly, therefore, I will rather
boast about my weaknesses, so that the
power of Christ may dwell in me
(2 Corinthians 12:9 NASB).

The shock of that day is still with me. Even now, I'm still processing the unthinkable.

My son's young wife—the mother of their baby boy was gone. She was taken in a freak farming accident. I could barely comprehend what was happening, yet I found myself called on for support. How could I be strong when I was so weak?

I was almost sixty years old and became the surrogate caregiver for a three-month-old baby. If anyone had suggested I was capable of the physical demands—much less the emotional ones—I was about to face, I would have laughed out loud. And yet, in a situation like that, God provides what we need when we need it. Not before, but there in the midst is where His strength is available.

Even as I tried to deny the reality of our situation, I knew where to turn. I ran to God. I burrowed into His word, starting my days early to read the Bible before the baby woke up. I used the sleepless parts of the nights to pray, and I journaled. I didn't take neat—refer to them later—notes from the passages I read in scripture. Instead, I chugged God's word like a thirsty woman gulps water. My prayers weren't orderly written in a prayer journal. These were honest times of searching and questioning— tear stained and ink-splotched. It was messy, but God used those hours to give me the strength to be what my family needed.

There's no right or wrong way to experience grief. But any grief struggle is better when we turn to God—first and frequently. I rediscovered He can handle my anger, my frustration, and my questions. He can bring peace in the worst of times, *if we let Him.*

During that time, I forged a bond with my Heavenly Father. Even now, I automatically reach for God's word before I get out of bed. It's one joy that has come from that horrific time.

An Honest Prayer When the Impossible Happens

For my thoughts are not your thoughts, neither
are your ways my ways," declares the Lord. As the
heavens are higher than the earth,
so are my ways higher than your ways
and my thoughts than your thoughts
(Isaiah 55:8-9 NIV)

Dear Lord, I cannot bear this. The unthinkable has happened, and I don't know how I can get through this. I need Your strength. And I need to understand.

How can You have allowed this? I prayed and begged You to take this from us and bring about a different ending. That didn't happen. Now I must continue to trust You even though it feels like You've let us down.

I shudder as I admit my fear and disappointment and anger.

If I tell You how I feel, will it affect how You treat my prayers in the future? Will it make You love me less? Even as these words cross my mind, I see what a lie they are. You love us. I know You are trustworthy, and You work in ways we cannot understand or even imagine … and yet here I am. Help me understand.

Give me Your strength to get through this. Show me how to reconcile this tragedy with how much I *know* You love us. Renew my trembling faith. I feel weak and unequipped to cope. Even in my doubt, You are the only refuge I have. Amen.

Creative Connection: The Power of Scribbles

Grief is inherently messy because grieving is bringing order back after chaos hits. Add emotions, along with an explosion of to-dos and we're deep in a place of feeling overwhelmed. And the only way out is through. We can't bypass the mourning process. All a sidestep does is postpone the pain and often make matters worse, not better. So, this creative connection is to help us embrace the chaos and get some of those messy pieces out so we can process them.

Supplies:
- [ ] This book
- [ ] Pen/Pencil
- [ ] Colored pencils/crayons/paint/colored pens

1. Begin by drawing a scribble. Leave some areas open—large enough to write a word.

2. In the spaces, write in words which describe what you're feeling. Don't judge the words that may come to mind. Some may seem oddly out of context. When I did this exercise after my dad passed away from a ten-year battle with Alzheimer's, the word I wrote was *relief*. I felt horribly guilty about that feeling, but when I wrote it down and explored what it meant, I realized I was relieved his suffering was over. Again, don't judge yourself.

3. Now ask God to show you something about each word. If you want to journal some of the insight you receive, that's fine!

4. Finally, color in the spaces. Use colors that reflect your mood.

Glimpses of the Impossible

Oh, Lord God! You Yourself made the heavens and earth by Your great power and with Your outstretched arm. Nothing is too difficult for You! (Jeremiah 32:17 HCSB).

The first time it happened, I was at the grocery store, doing my impression of life-as-usual while searching for a new normal in the everyday tasks of life. I had rounded the end of one aisle when a woman pushing a buggy turned the corner at the other end. The sight of her stopped me in my tracks. It was an impossibility, but the blonde bob and the way she moved reminded me so strongly of Jennifer my heart skipped a beat. At that moment in time, the authorities hadn't yet located my friend's body, but they had come to the inescapable assumption she'd been murdered.

I knew the woman I'd seen couldn't be her, but I had to have confirmation. Trying to be subtle, I stalked that poor woman through the store. It took several moments before I saw her face-to-face. The eyes that met mine weren't those of my friend, only of a puzzled woman who obviously wondered why I was following her.

I smiled with non-threatening reassurance and fled. I abandoned my cart and almost ran to car—thankful I was alone. There I gave in to the storm of tears and argued with God about the unfairness of my loss.

Despite all the facts, I wanted my friend to still be alive. Beyond that, I realized I'd been unconsciously searching for her everywhere I went. I knew God could make the impossible a reality, and that was what I begged Him for—to no avail. A week later, they uncovered her body in a landfill near where she'd been murdered.

Time passed and slowly, my plea for the impossible-made-possible changed. Instead of asking for Him to return Jennifer to us, I asked for the ability to move past the debilitating grief of her loss. In some ways, that request seemed harder for God to do than the first prayer.

But this was the prayer He answered.

He didn't answer it all in one moment. Instead, the healing came in little moments, almost imperceptibly at first, then gathering momentum. God can and will do the impossible, but He gets to choose which impossible gift to give us. For me, it was a new life—my new life. And with that blessing, I learned no matter what prayer God answers, it's always crammed full of unexpected blessings.

A Prayer Asking for the Impossible

I know that You can do all things, And that no
purpose of Yours can be thwarted
(Job 42:2 NIV).

Dear Lord, I know I'm asking for the impossible. I want this nightmare of loss to be a bad dream. Let me wake up tomorrow and find my loved one back where she belongs. I don't want to walk this path alone.

Your word promises all things are possible with you. And yet, I know You get to decide which impossibilities You attack. Why can't I accept this? Am I selfish to want her back? I know she's in a better place, and that's supposed to be comforting, but I don't feel comforted.

Perhaps I'm asking You to work on the wrong miracle. Maybe I'm the one who needs new life. I feel dead to everything except pain. Even though it hasn't been nearly long enough, I want out of this dark place. Is that the selfish prayer? Asking to move on doesn't that mean I don't value who she was and all she meant to me.

I'm so tired and confused. Please take my struggle and make it go away. Give me peace and rest from this burden of sorrow. Replace it with the ability to once again enjoy life and serve You in a way that honors her memory. Lord, You are my strength. Show me how to allow that strength to flow through me and get me past this struggle. Amen.

Creative Connection; Doing the Impossible

If you're like me—and others I know—you probably have at least one thing you haven't done because of the grief you're experiencing. We're going to remedy that omission with this creative connection.

Supplies
- [ ] This book
- [ ] Pen
- [ ] Colored pencils
- [ ] Tape and photos to decorate this page

Begin by considering something that grief has prevented you from doing. Something big, like a vacation. Or something small, like going out to dinner. Whatever it is, write it on this page.

Now ask God to accomplish the impossible.

What you write should fall into one of these two categories. Here's what to do next:

☐ A Small Thing: For this option, go do it. Then come back here and journal how you felt. Include how you felt before and the emotions you felt afterward.

☐ A Big Thing: For this option, use this space to brainstorm how to make this activity happen. Then take the first step. Now journal how you felt before and what you feel now that you've begun.

Letting Go of What If

*If then you have been raised with Christ, seek the
things that are above, where Christ is, seated at
the right hand of God. ² Set your minds on things
that are above, not on things that are on earth*
(Colossians 3:1-2 ESV).

I'm a big one to visit the world of what if—especially when I'm grappling with major life changes. The pandemic and shelter at home orders of 2020 have been difficult for me. I return to the what-ifs of 2020. And like a hall of mirrors gone wrong, all I see are reflections of what I expected and what didn't happen.

I had a lot of expectations. Our first two grandsons were born this year. We're blessed beyond measure because both families live within a few miles of us. This year should have been much gathering together—strengthening family and friendships. Instead, I watched my kids struggle to become new parents in isolation.

Everything was different—from the baby showers to the births. All the physical gatherings were different—and sparse. Only meetups, phone calls, Facetime, and cell phone pictures. Not the way I envisioned welcoming my grandchildren into this world.

This could have been such a great year if only …

Instead of focusing on all the goodness of this year, I rehearsed unmet expectations and the experiences I missed.

None of which was helpful in the least.

The more I dwelt on what didn't happen, the more depressed I became. Finally, as I was writing a new keynote presentation, God got my attention. He reminded me He was in control of this year, and He'd populated it with unbelievable blessings—which I was currently downplaying or ignoring altogether.

Both my daughters-in-law had healthy pregnancies with few issues beyond the normal difficulties. Both grandsons were born healthy—with their fathers in attendance. And while we've practiced more safety issues than any other grandparents before this year, we've been included as an important part of both family groups. And these are just the tip of the blessing iceberg.

I'm so grateful God is patient with me and redirected my mental path.

This was the crux of the keynote I delivered with an attitude of thanksgiving and hope that the worst was behind us. I returned home from the conference on Sunday and then on Monday, we lost our daughter-in-law in a tragic farm accident.

I had to decide if I believed God would bring good out of bad, peace out of chaos, and joy out of sorrow. And I had to find a way to stay out of the trap of *what-if*.

I'm far too familiar with this land of what-if-make-believe. I've visited many times during my life. I know the landscape of haunted valleys and mazes of punishing practices. I recognize them for their futility, and yet it's the first place I head when life turns upside down.

I *am* spending less time there now because I'm quicker to recognize the dreary scenery and leave. But it's taken years to understand the path out of that place is a journey of faith.

Faith has many different faces and applications. One of them is the ability to believe God is still in control—even when circumstances turn out in a way we wish they hadn't. So, as I once again process the loss of life, I'm chose to draw close to God, instead of spending time in the land of *what if*.

A Prayer Asking for God to Deliver Me From What If

Yet God has made everything beautiful for its own time. He has planted eternity in the human heart, but even so, people cannot see the whole scope of God's work from beginning to end (Ecclesiastes 3:11 NLT).

Dear Lord, You are sovereign, and You know the end from the beginning. Yet I act as if I don't believe this foundational truth. I'm once again mired in the bog of what-if, and it's sucking me under. Help me focus on You and leave this dreary place.

I'm such a control freak, and yet, I'm finding no comfort in the false belief that I can control the world around me. I wanted this time of life to have turned out differently. I wanted the path I expected.

Since I can't have my way, I want to understand why life had to change so drastically. Chasing that answer is leading me into the make-believe world of what if. Everywhere I turn, I'm bombarded by the lie that says I could have changed the way it happened. Help me, Lord, to understand my part in this. Show me the intersection of truth—where Your sovereignty and my free will meet.

I'm afraid I'll never understand, and that lack of understanding will keep me from peace. Help me seek my peace in You and You alone. Keep me from the nightmares of what if and cover me with your wings of love. Amen.

Creative Connection: Letting Go

It's easy to hold on to thoughts and emotions long after they're useful to us. Today we're going to practice letting go.

Supplies
- ☐ This book
- ☐ Pen
- ☐ Colored pencils
- ☐ Decoration for this page

Ask God to show you what He wants you to turn over to Him. Then use the letters in the phrase below to make an acrostic, adding words and phrases describing what you are ready to leave behind.

LETTING

GO

Waiting for Sunrise

The Lord is good to those who wait for him,
to the soul who seeks him
(Lamentations 3:25 ESV).

We go to the beach a couple of times a year and my favorite time is on the beach when the sun rises, taking pictures. I also love watching the birds who hang out on and around the shore.

One year, the reason for being at the beach was to attend the memorial service of a close friend who had passed away. Although it was good to remember him with others who loved him, the trip was hard and the time I spent on the beach was more therapeutic than joyful. But during one of my early morning walks, God revealed a comforting truth.

As I watched the sun come up, I noticed how the birds gathered with me to watch the day begin. As I considered them, I realized birds always congregated whenever I've watched the sun rise. At the beach, they gather on the shore, many of them swooping in to land just a few minutes before the sun made its daily debut. In the mountains, they perch in the trees. And at the lake, they gather on the dock.

The birds gather for sunrise, but it doesn't matter what the weather is like. The birds still come. It can be cloudless or completely overcast. It makes no difference. Those faithful avians still wait and watch the sunrise. Once the sun is up (and sometimes I can only tell it's risen by my watch and the overall lightening of the sky) they disperse, winging away to their daily duties.

That day it occurred to me that the sunrise in my life was obscured—not by clouds—but by grief. Yet I knew God was still with me, no matter whether I saw Him working or not. And it was time to put action to my faith and—just like those birds—turn to where I knew He was. There's no doubt it's easier to walk with God when we can see a physical sign that He's on the horizon. Even when grief makes us feel like everyone—including God has deserted us—we still must find the faith to face the dawn. Mourning can fill life with gloomy clouds until we're no longer able to discern where God is or when He's going to begin the work we can see. It's during those times when we must rely on what we *know* is true about God instead of relying on what we're feeling.

So that day, as I watched the sunrise behind a wall of clouds, I renewed my commitment to faith—God is *always* at work whether or not I see Him. He is always present, even when my circumstances hide Him from my view.

A Prayer About Watching for the Light

The light shines in the darkness, and the darkness has not overcome it
(John 1:5 ESV).

Dear Lord, sometimes my world feels so dark. I miss my loved one so much. And truthfully, I don't want to live in the light. All I want to do is curl up in a corner and wait to join them.

My world feels different, and I don't want to live this life. I want to go back and continue with all I had planned. Help me see purpose in the path ahead.

But You have a purpose for me, a hope and a reason for me to continue. I need to see a glimmer of what that is. I need a new spark in my cold heart.

Help me draw nearer to You during this difficult time. Warm me with the flame of Your love and renew my hope. I feel Your love. I know You've been with me through all of this. Remind me of Your loving care.

Lead me to once again to watching for the light.

Creative Connection: A New Day

Whether you're grieving the loss of a person or a losing situation, it's time to move forward. We're going to start that by watching the sun rise.

For years, I was a night owl and rarely got up—on purpose—to watch the sun make its first appearance of the day. That habit has changed and more and more my day begins just before the sun peeks over the horizon.

Supplies
- ☐ This book
- ☐ Pen
- ☐ Camera (optional)

I embrace this morning ritual, and I'd like for you to try it—at least once. Here's what to do:

1. The night before your sunrise, determine when the sun is due to rise and set your alarm about fifteen to thirty minutes before that time.

2. On the morning of your sunrise, get up and pull on some clothes that will be weather appropriate for the time of year.

3. Either walk outside or get in your car and drive to a scenic spot where you will view the sunrise.

4. Now sit in silence as the miracle of the new day unfolds. Notice the surrounding sounds. Do you hear or see the birds? What else do you observe.

5. Next, ask God to give you some insight and encouragement about this new path He's allowed you to walk. Journal what He says and remember to record any Bible verses that come to mind.

6. Finally, if you have a camera nearby, snap a picture or two of this new day dawning.

When Life Turns You Upside Down

*But as for you, be strong and do not give
up, for your work will be rewarded*
(2 Chronicles 15:7 NIV).

Hubby and I had the chance to sneak away for a day to play. Even though it was crazy hot, the getaway was just what we needed. The time away also gave me the opportunity to take some butterfly pics. I love their vibrant colors and graceful movements. But I also saw qualities about them, which I can apply to my life.

First, they were single-minded in their pursuit of nectar. As I watched, several butterflies successfully ran off bees and other trespassers as they flitted from flower to flower. They didn't allow any distraction to keep them from their focus.

Next, I saw how the gusty wind frequently forced them to cling to branches from awkward positions. They worked hard to stay connected to the blossoms where they received nourishment. But they stayed in place, even when the breeze turned them upside down.

I also noticed how my presence in their midst didn't deter them. They kept their distance but worked around me without disrupting their activities.

Watching these beautiful insects in their single-minded pursuit of purpose inspired me. Before this I'd always considered butterflies delicate, but that day I saw a different side to them—tenacious, single-minded, and capable no matter the circumstances.

Life circumstances disrupt my focus and pull me from what I'm called to do. I'm easily distracted and far from single-minded in following God's path for my life. I also allow upsetting circumstances to blow me off my path, instead of learning how to hang on and continue with my goal. I let others stand in my way—particularly if I see them as a giant in what I'm endeavoring.

My bottom line is this, I'm going to learn how to hang on and extract every bit of sweetness and purpose from today, even if the world turns me upside down.

A Prayer When Life Tilts

Now may the Lord of peace himself give you peace at all times in every way. The Lord be with you all (2 Thessalonians 3:16 ESV).

Dear Lord, life has tilted again, and I feel like I'm clinging by a thread. Everything is upside down and out of kilter. I desperately want circumstances to be different, but I have no control. Help me once again find my footing on solid ground.

I'm searching for normalcy in a world that is no longer normal.

You have always been my foundation, but I'm frozen in place and uncertain which way to reach out to feel a connection to You. Take my hand and wrap me in your loving embrace. Make me safe once again.

Reassure me of my purpose in this topsy-turvy reality. Remind me of the last words You told me so I can once again find the Your path. You are my anchor in this storm-tossed world, and I know You are worthy of my faith.

You have disappointed no one who calls You Lord. Calm my anxious thoughts and renew my peace even as You're growing my faith. Amen.

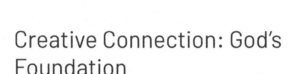

Creative Connection: God's Foundation

Grief often leaves us with a wobbly foundation. Everything in life appears to have shifted, and it can leave us wondering what is real and what is true. Today, you're going to rebuild that foundation using Scripture.

Supplies
- [ ] This book
- [ ] Pen
- [ ] Bible or Bible app
- [ ] Colored pencils
- [ ] Index cards, small notebook, or similar scraps of paper

Below are a few Bible verses to help you get started. But I want this foundation to be specific to *you*. I know God will give you exactly what you need.

Writing out Bible verses has helped me most during my grieving process. When I'm grieving, my mind isn't firing on all cylinders and that means my memory is unreliable. So, I carry my list of God's foundation words with me to help me remember He is a solid rock on which to rebuild my life.

Once you have the Bible verses, put them in a form that you can carry with you. You could write them on index cards and string them on a metal ring or purchase a small book or notepad and record them there. The idea is to have them with you so that when the world shifts, or you begin to once again doubt God's foundation, they're within easy reach.

☐ Psalm 30:5

☐ Nahum 1:7

☐ Isaiah 43:3

☐ Matthew 5:4

☐ John 16:33

☐ Romans 8:35

Scripture Prescriptions

Prescription 1

*For I know the plans I have for you, declares
the Lord, plans for welfare and not for
evil, to give you a future and a hope*
(Jeremiah 29:11 ESV).

Prescription 2

*Call on Me in a day of trouble; I will
rescue you, and you will honor Me*
(Psalm 50:15 HCSB).

Prescriptions 3

*I can do all this through him who gives me
strength* (Philippians 4:13 NIV).

Chapter Two

Letting Go of Anger And Choosing Peace

I don't know about you, but I dislike change—any kind of change. And there's nothing more life-changing than loss. When life shifts, I fight against the change and often battle anger and sadness.

Letting go of the anger that erupts when circumstances are different is difficult for me. But for my peace of mind—and for those close to me, I try to be aware of how loss can push me toward anger and try to deliberately choose peace instead. Sometimes I'm more successful than other times.

While it helps to know that anger is a normal part of the grieving process, I've had to make sure I was not using this knowledge as an excuse to indulge my feelings. The anger I battle comes from several places, especially my lack of control.

I know control is more of perception than reality, yet I cling to it like a lifeline. When I lose someone I love or the world shifts direction, I realize again I wasn't in control after all.

Acknowledging my lack of control is only the first step. Knowing I'm not in charge doesn't really bring me any peace at all. But the next step—acknowledging Who is in control does.

Nothing catches God off guard. He exists outside of time and is everywhere—and every-when—simultaneously. When I stay close by His side, protected by His love, I can weather any storm of loss or change that the world throws my way.

Surrounded by God's People

Carry one another's burdens; in this way
you will fulfill the law of Christ
(Galatians 6:2 HCSB)

We lived with our son on their farm for three months after he lost his wife. Even though it was only a few miles from our home, farm life differed from our busy subdivision On the farm, the healing presence of nature insulated and surrounded us. I never tired of watching the deer. A lot of farmers consider deer nuisance animals, but my daughter-in-law loved them. Hunting was never allowed on their property.

Every morning and every evening, they'd congregate in the field near the house. I didn't notice this habit initially because they were half hidden by the tall grasses and moved with a stealthy grace. After my son pointed them out, I watched for their daily appearances.

The only time they were easy to spot was when something alarmed them. Then their heads snapped up, and if spooked further, they'd bound away. When this happened, I was always surprised by how many of them there were.

As I watched this occurrence one evening, a parallel hit me. These deer were like the community that had surrounded us during that difficult time. When we lost Katie, there was an immediate outpouring of help. People we'd not noticed for years appeared in our lives and rushed toward us with the assistance we needed.

God's people are ever vigilant. As we move away from the tragedy, I realize I'm part of that watchful community. I'm less the recipient and once again part of the watchful herd, ready to step in when there's a need. The family of God may not always be visible, but they are there when we need them, ready to spring into action when called upon.

A Prayer Asking For the Presence of God's People

Your abundance at the present time should supply their need, so that their abundance may supply your need, that there may be fairness (2 Corinthians 8:14 ESV).

Dear Lord, I need Your help. I'm drowning in tears and I'm desperately alone. I know it's my fault. I've pushed away those who offered to walk through this with me.

In my pride, I thought I could do this. I was certain I didn't need anyone else. I was wrong. I need others to help me process what I'm dealing with. Beyond that, grief is clogging my mind. What seemed clear and simple is now difficult to accomplish.

Give me the courage to reach out to those who offered to help. Don't let me be too proud to ask for the assistance I need. I know You've put me amid a community for a reason. Forgive me for not accepting the help You provided and give me the opportunity to change my mind.

Bring people back into my life with offers to help. I promise I'll accept this time. You've been so patient and so loving. You've provided everything I needed—even before I knew I needed it. Thank You for loving me so much. Amen.

Creative Connection: A Letter of Appreciation

Today we're going to write a letter. It's not exactly a thank you note. And truthfully, this note is one you'll never mail. In this season of grief, I challenge you to write a letter telling God how much you appreciate all He's done for you.

Supplies

☐ This book
☐ Pen
☐ Writing paper

When I lost my daughter-in-law, this was a letter I did *not* want to write. I was angry and resentful toward God because He allowed her to die and leave an infant and my son behind. Nothing about that situation felt fair or just. And I didn't want to acknowledge that God could do anything worth appreciating.

But this exercise helped me heal and move past that anger. Writing a letter like this helped me see that even in these impossible circumstances, God still had good gifts to give and was providing what we needed.

You can write your letter here in this book or on another piece of paper. But do it and let God replace anger with peace.

Finding a New Focus and Reconnecting

Praise the God and Father of our Lord Jesus Christ, the Father of mercies and the God of all comfort (2 Corinthians 1:3 HCSB).

My dad was a professional landscape photographer. His specialty was taking black and white photographs. As the oldest of two, I was the one who got to accompany him on his early morning excursions when we traveled.

As I got into my teens, going with dad on those early morning trips became less attractive. I was like so many other teenagers—way too cool for my parents. Daddy always offered to bring me along but didn't chastise me when I turned him down.

As a married woman, young mother, and busy business owner, I never found the time to hang out with him while he was taking pictures. A couple of times he mentioned how he'd love to pass his love of photography on to me, but I never found the time to take him up on his offer.

Now it's too late.

Daddy is in heaven, and I'm left with a hole in my heart filled only with regret. For a while after Daddy passed, I avoided my camera. It felt wrong to pick it up now that it was too late. I told myself that I'd made my bed—and the wrong decision—and I had to live with the consequences.

But the pull toward the camera was too strong, so I timidly experimented. Slowly, I dug out information from blogs, magazines, books, and even online classes and honed my skill as a photographer. Something amazing happened.

Instead of feeling worse because I'd missed this connection point while Daddy was still with me, I reconnected with him. Memories came alive as I understood his passion.

I hadn't missed it. He *had* passed on much of his love of photography to me. I just had to be courageous enough to explore. The deeper I got into photography, the more I reconnected with him and with precious times we'd spent together.

I got to know him in ways I never had before.

I also realized that my relationship with my heavenly father is like this, too. So often I look at the missed opportunities and believe God's timing has passed me by. But He's still there—hands outstretched—with an open invitation to join Him.

Prayer About Regrets

The thief comes only to steal and kill and destroy.
I came that they may have life and have it
abundantly (John 10:10 ESV).

Dear Lord, it's so hard to get past the regrets I carry with me. I don't know how to set them aside and move forward. Will You help me?

In some ways, I don't want to leave them behind. They feel like a burden I deserve to carry. I should have known better, done better, been better. This is the guilt I ought to carry to make up for past mistakes.

But I don't see anything in Your holy Word that tells me I should continue to punish myself. Everywhere I see how You created us for joy and to live an abundant life. I yearn for that abundance, but I'm mired in the past and saddled with poor choices. Help me move forward.

Show me how to reconnect with my now-absent loved one. Bring to my mind memories that flood my heart with joy. Help me recapture moments I thought were lost.

Lead me out of this place of self-inflicted punishment and back into the light of Your presence. Amen.

Creative Connection: Reconnect

One of the most confusing parts of grief is sorting through all the emotions. Today, we're going to begin looking at all the conflicting emotions that have invaded our lives with this season of grief.

Supplies
- ☐ This book
- ☐ Pen
- ☐ Colored pencils
- ☐ Decorations for this page

Answer the questions below and get ready for the surprising insights God will show you.

- ☐ I miss this about my loved one …

- ☐ My favorite memory is…

☐   I regret …

☐   I feel best when I think about …

☐   I'm afraid when I think about …

☐   What God is showing me right now …

Peace in the Midst of a Storm

*I have told you these things, so that in
me you may have peace. In this world
you will have trouble. But take heart!
I have overcome the world*
(John 16:33 NIV).

In addition to being an author, I'm also a photographer. This past winter, I visited our local downtown during a snowstorm to take pictures. I love visiting this area. There's a river and a waterfall and an amazing pedestrian suspension bridge overlooking it all.

I spent a couple of hours capturing images of snow. At one place on the bridge, there's a tulip tree and on this day, the dead blossoms were partially filled with snow, giving them an ethereal feel. Add a blue gray leaden sky and there were some amazing photo opportunities.

After I got home and downloaded my images, I found one I loved. I pulled it from the multitude and immediately titled it, "Peace."

To me, everything about it whispered peace. It conjured up a setting where delicate snowflakes drift down in a quiet forest. Looking at the picture, I could almost hear the silence. And truthfully, that was how I *felt* while taking this picture. By focusing on this small slice of the whole, my entire soul felt the breath of peace waft through it.

The circumstances surrounding that image were as far from peaceful as a person could get. I was standing on a suspension bridge over a flood-raging river with crowds around me. Instead of delicate flakes, snow fell in a blizzard of large wet clumps. My gloves were soaked, and my hands were numb. Beyond that, because I was on a bridge, the slush beneath my feet was freezing, and I was terrified I might slip on the ice and fall. I must have taken dozens of pictures to get one in focus because of the wind and the crowds. The bridge shook like a trampoline.

So why choose that title?

I chose it because true peace, the internal kind that carries supernatural calm, isn't dependent on my circumstances. In my spirit that day, I walked away from the chaos of my surroundings and returned renewed and recharged.

When I lose someone I love, I stagger in a blizzard of fear and uncertainty—heart and hands frozen with a bleak-seeming future. But I've learned to return to the truth of this experience. Peace doesn't come to us *because* of circumstances, it comes to us *in the midst* of circumstances.

And as much as our tragedy caught us off guard, it did not catch God by surprise. Only God knows the reason behind the why and when of death. But when we know God—and put our trust in Him—we can find the peace that supersedes anything we face.

A Prayer for Peace in Spite of Circumstances

He is not afraid of bad news; his heart is firm, trusting in the Lord (Psalm 112:7 ESV).

Dear Lord, I know I can put my trust in You, but grief makes belief so hard. I want to trust You and Your timing, but I wanted longer with my loved one. And the fact that he's now gone leaves me unbalanced and my soul unquiet.

Help me move past my circumstances and back into the solid foundation of Your peace. Quiet my emotions and fill me with the unexplainable presence of Your Spirit. Remind me of Your love—for me and for my loved one. Don't let me forget all the ways You've shown Your love to me.

Don't let me become bitter and cold. Instead, rekindle a fire in my heart and allow me to love again without fear. It's so hard to lose someone I love. It makes me want to insulate myself from future hurt by encasing my heart in ice.

Take away the fear and replace it with trust. You are worthy of my trust, and I thank You for loving us. Amen.

Creative Connection: Weathering Grief

This exercise will help you forecast the weather in your life right now and look ahead to what's ahead.

Supplies
- [ ] This book
- [ ] Pen
- [ ] Colored pencils
- [ ] Decorations for this page

Begin by reading this verse and asking God to reveal the weather forecast in your life right now.

Then they cried to the Lord in their trouble, and he delivered them from their distress. He made the storm be still, and the waves of the sea were hushed. Then they were glad that the waters were quiet, and he brought them to their desired haven. Let them thank the Lord for his steadfast love, for his wondrous works to the children of man! (Psalm 107: 28-31 ESV).

What does your life feel like right now? A thunderstorm, a dreary day, rain with the sun shining, fog or something else?

Divide the space on this page in half (horizontally or vertically, it doesn't matter).

On the first half, put a representation of the weather you feel now. You can use pictures from a magazine, pictures you take yourself, or draw what you're experiencing.

On the second half, put a representation of the weather you'd like to experience. Again, use pictures or a drawing.

Finding Spiritual Peace in Nature

*But ask the animals, and they will teach
you, or the birds in the sky, and they will
tell you; or speak to the earth, and it will teach
you, or let the fish in the sea inform you*
(Job 12:7-8 NIV).

Where do you go when life overwhelms you?
That's an important question to ask and to answer. While the ultimate—best—answer is always God. We all have different places that help us find Him more easily. Some search out a quiet corner, others find Him in a church building.

For me, the place that ushers me into the presence of God is the out-of-doors, surrounded by nature. Refocusing on the unexpected beauty found in God's creation gives me the perspective and peace I crave when life crashes around me. It's my first choice of places to run when I'm grieving.

Being out in God's creation grounds me and reminds me of certain truths I've forgotten or ignored during my grief.

> 1) Life has rhythm. Seasons change, flowers bloom, and birds still sing—even when I'm grieving. I need the reminder that life continues during my calamity.
>
> 2) God doesn't change or disappear. Even though life has a rhythm, God is always the same. He's always present and always at work. When I take the time to look up from my circumstances, He's there to be found.
>
> 3) God loves us. His creation provides the proof of God's love to me. I find it in the beauty He's created as well as His exquisite attention to detail.

When loss overwhelms me, I escape to the fields and the mountains. There I drink in the spiritual truths illustrated in the natural world. I spend time with God. And in nature, I let Him soothe my soul and restore my peace.

A Prayer for God to Give Me Peace in My Grief

In his hand is the life of every creature and the breath of all mankind (Job 12: 10 NIV).

Dear Lord, You are always the answer I seek when life crashes around me. My soul is heavy, and my eyes burn from all the tears I've shed. I want to feel something other than grief, but my sadness has pushed out every other emotion.

Nothing in life is as it should be. My routine is gone, and even my purpose seems to have evaporated. I want to feel close to You, but even Your presence is hard to find. Show me the way back to Your side. Return my peace during my turmoil.

Let me have eyes to recognize You in the world around me. Show me your love in the flowers and the trees. Sing over me with the sweet voices of Your birds. Teach me to recognize the rhythm that is still present in the world today. Remind me life and death are part of the life you've given us here on earth. Most of all, help me remember that death isn't the end, but only the beginning.

I know You love me and are here with me. Let me feel Your loving touch and begin the healing process as I rejoin life on the other side of loss. Amen.

Creative Connection: Create a Grief Page

A grief page sounds like a downer, but it's never been for me. Praying before starting the page keeps it positive. Before you begin, ask God to use this exercise to begin/continue the healing process. Let Him show you unexpected feelings, memories, and insights.

Supplies:

☐ This book

☐ Newspaper, magazines, decorative paper—anything with words & images printed on it. This is a place to consider using some of the condolence cards you've received. You don't have to, but some of us keep them and toss them later.

☐ Glue stick

☐ Scissors

☐ Pen
☐ Colored pencils
☐ Stickers

Begin by cutting out words and images that appeal to you. Don't limit yourself, just cut. After you have a good bit of ephemeral, go through it and arrange it on the page. When you're happy with the arrangement, use the glue stick to put it into place. You can also add other items like a bird feather, a piece of lace, or part of a note from someone.

As you assemble this, ask God to bring a Bible verse to your mind. Write the reference or copy the entire verse somewhere on the page.

Sometimes Endings Can Bring Peace

Brothers and sisters, we do not want you
to be uninformed about those who sleep
in death, so that you do not grieve like
the rest of mankind, who have no hope
(1 Thessalonians 4:13 NIV).

Hubby and I love to hike. Last year we visited a new vista in the Blue Ridge Mountains, Craggy Pinnacle, to watch the sunset. Even though the clouds hid the sun itself, the colors were magnificent—intense reds and oranges contrasted with soft blues and purples. It was a feast for the eyes.

We stayed on top of that mountain until the last of the light faded. Our unwillingness to leave meant we then had to face a treacherous climb down the mountain in the dark—with only a tiny flashlight to guide us. But it was worth every perilous step.

Those moments were beautiful and precious. That time we spent together is a memory. We can revisit the pictures I took and reminisce about the experience, but it's over. There's an important lesson for me here. Life is a process of beginnings and endings—many of them beautiful and filled with peace if we'll only open our senses to the experience.

I've had the privilege of being present when several loved ones moved from this life into eternity. For some, the process was a difficult struggle. For others, they slipped from one place into the other without a whisper. But there has been one constant with each passing. When my loved one was gone, peace remained.

There was also great sorrow, but under it was a foundation of unexpected peace.

After each loss came a difficult time, just like that climb down the mountain. But God's light is always the constant we need that will lead us to safety if we'll only let Him.

To live life fully, I've learned I must appreciate the *nows* of life. Nothing stays the same, but almost all of it can bring beauty and peace if we'll only appreciate the moments and linger long enough to see it.

A Prayer About Endings

The light shines in the darkness, and the
darkness has not overcome it
(John 1:5 ESV).

Dear Lord, I didn't want to say goodbye to my precious loved one. I wanted life to continue with him in my life. Now my world seems much darker and unfamiliar. Paths I once walked without a single hesitation now make me stumble. Help me find my footing again.

Show me how to navigate this difficult ending without giving up completely. Reveal the moments of peace that accompanied this time of loss. Bring memories of joy and beauty to my mind.

Illuminate my steps as I walk into a new season. I didn't choose this, but I know You are with me. Let me feel Your hand clasping mine, providing stability and peace. You were always the constant in my life, no matter what I faced. I know this won't change because You will never change.

You love me and You love those I care for. Give me peace in the midst of this grief-filled time. I want to get past the intense sense of loss, but I know even that pain has purpose. Don't let me rush past the time I need. Insulate me from the judgment of others as I heal with You. You are all I need. Amen.

Creative Connection: Letting God Repair What's Broken

What is broken in your life? What doors have you slammed shut because of the grief you've been feeling? Today, we're going to let God heal what's broken.

Supplies
- [ ] This book
- [ ] Pen
- [ ] Colored pencils
- [ ] Tape, stickers, and objects to decorate this page

This will be an ongoing exercise and I encourage you to keep with it because God has some amazing healing in store for you!

- [ ] First, list several areas that are broken and parts of your mind/life you've cut off.

☐ After you have your list, look at it and assign each item a color.

☐ Now use a scrap piece of paper and draw circles on it. In each circle, write something from your list. Then color that circle the color you assigned it. Do this on only one side of each circle.

☐ Next, pray over the circles and cut them out. Put a hole in each one and thread them on a long piece of string.

☐ Now take an old key and write the word GOD on it.

☐ Add the key to the string. Tie the string so nothing falls off.

☐ As God repairs and replaces what's broken, write it on the blank side of each circle.

☐ Hang the key up somewhere you can see it and let it remind you that God can open any door and restore anything you've lost.

Scripture Prescriptions

Prescription 1

Surely God is my salvation; I will trust and not be afraid. The Lord, the Lord himself, is my strength and my defense; he has become my salvation (Isaiah 12:2 NIV).

Prescription 2

In peace I will both lie down and sleep, For You alone, Lord, have me dwell in safety. (Psalm 4:8 NASB)

Prescription 3

Now may the God of peace himself sanctify you completely, and may your whole spirit and soul and body be kept blameless at the coming of our Lord Jesus Christ (1 Thessalonians 5:23 ESV).

Chapter Three

Learning to Live with What Cannot be Changed

Expectations.

That one word is a minefield for so many of us. When expectations are met—for the most part—we consider life good. But when they're not, our lives come crashing down in a hurry. And grief is intimately tied up in our expectations. We expect to have more time with loved ones, a financial outlook that continues to improve, and a positive work situation. Expectations encompass every aspect of life, from relationships to the weather.

And we have expectations about God.

When I was a newer believer, I used to approach God like an algebra equation. If I had all the correct variables, I could solve for peace and joy. If one of my variables was off, I'd fix it, and life would get back on track. On the surface, this thought process looked good. But when I dug deeper, I realized that rather than finding God's truth in the equation, I'd become tangled in a lie.

I had attempted to dumb down God.

God is so much more than a solvable equation. His love destroys such a simplistic concept and replaces it with grace.

Along with His love and grace come conditions I can't understand—good people who suffer and bad people who are granted eternal life. It seems as if rewards go to cheaters and punishment to those who do right.

But I don't have to understand Him to trust Him.

I find evidence for hope all around me. I've seen it played out in my life and in the lives of those around me. I've seen it in the kindness of strangers, the provision of friends and love of neighbors during a catastrophe. I've watched a lifelong alcoholic, who lost everything and everyone, spend her remaining years making sure no one else walked that road alone. I've seen a husband forgive a wife and rebuild a marriage into a witness and a beacon of what God can do. Most of all, I've seen God show up again and again with the provision we desperately need—before we even know to ask. Every page of the Bible is full of hope. God proves He gives us so much more than the condemnation that we deserve.

Peace with the Plan B

*And we know that God causes all things to work
together for good to those who love God, to
those who are called according to His purpose*
(Romans 8:28 NASB).

I was so excited to be back at one of my favorite mountain getaways—in a new season. As the leader of a retreat, I had built in some photography side trips, and I was looking forward to sneaking away. Normally, I spend a little time researching an area the evening before I go out for sunrise shots. But because I was familiar with the area, I didn't. I couldn't have been more wrong.

I crawled out of bed, pulling on warm clothes in the dark so I wouldn't wake my husband, and slipped out of the room. On the top floor, a community room had a balcony perfect for capturing the sun rising in the notch between two mountains.

As the sky began to glow with the upcoming sun, I could tell something was off. I'd forgotten a basic law of the universe. The sun doesn't rise in the same spot every day of the year. I would not get the picture I wanted from this view. There wasn't time to go to a different spot, so I decided to tough it out and see what happened.

The scene *was* beautiful. The sun didn't rise where I expected, but the new perspective provided gorgeous pictures. And the experience taught me a valuable life lesson.

I recalibrated my vision of Plan B.

I've always considered Plan B as something less. An arrangement I would make do with, but not ideal. Settling for a second choice always made me sad because it implied I was getting less than I'd planned.

That conclusion couldn't have been farther from the truth. My balcony experience revealed that Plan B isn't always second best. And in the terms for God's will in our lives—God doesn't have a Plan B. His plans for us always come to pass.

Sometimes living with the unexpected is painful, especially when we're suffering a loss of someone we love or an unexpected failure or defeat. But God is true to His word, and He always brings good out of bad.

A Prayer When Life is Different

*So be strong and courageous! Do not be afraid
and do not panic before them. For the Lord
your God will personally go ahead of you. He will
neither fail you nor abandon you.*
(Deuteronomy 31:6 NLT)

Dear Lord, this trouble is not what I wanted or expected. I had great plans and now they're all in chaos. How could You let this happen?

Forgive me for being upset with You, but I'm so sad. You could have stopped this—saved my loved one, yet You chose not to. Help me understand.

I know You love me. Your scripture tells me You plan only the best for me. How can this be the best? I'm lonely, hurt, and almost without hope. How do I pick up the pieces of my life?

You are all I have left. You are where I'm going to start. You promise to be here for me, and I'm holding You to Your word. I can rest because You *are* trustworthy. Bring to my mind all You've done for me, all the ways You've provided for me when life came apart at the seams in the past. Remind me of Your goodness and Your love.

Don't let me fall into despair. Instead, draw me close and whisper Your love into my withered heart. Renew my hope and give me the strength to search for good in the midst of this difficulty.

You will never leave or forsake me. Even in my grief, I feel Your presence. Never let me go, no matter what. Amen.

Creative Connection: An Alternative Timeline

Grief forces us off the path we'd planned and onto a different one. Sometimes it means traveling without someone we love. It may mean letting go of circumstances that will never come to pass.

Supplies
- ☐ This book
- ☐ Pen
- ☐ Colored pencils
- ☐ Items to decorate this page

Today we're going to anticipate what life may look like as we move forward on a different journey.

- ☐ Being by writing what you think your future would have looked like if the loss hadn't happened. You can be as general or specific as you'd like.

☐ Next, ask God to give you His insight into what possibilities lie ahead as you travel this new path.

☐ Write about how events and relationships could happen with this new reality. It's okay if they're negative as well as positive. This isn't an exercise in blind optimism. As negative thoughts come to your mind, ask God to give you alternatives. Record these insights and choices as well.

I Didn't Want to Go Back In

But the Helper, the Holy Spirit, whom the Father
will send in my name, he will teach you all things
and bring to your remembrance all that I have
said to you (John 14:26 ESV).

We were spending a rare night at our house when the midnight call came. I saw the caller's name and picture, slipped out of bed, and answered on the way down the stairs. My close friend's nineteen-year-old son had been in an auto accident and was in the operating room, undergoing emergency surgery. It had only been a couple of months since our daughter-in-law's accident, and I didn't want to walk this path again, not even for a friend.

Life doesn't always give us options.

Even though I wasn't with my friend, I recognized the place where she found herself. The words she spoke, the feelings she shared, and the fear she felt were so familiar—and the pain so recent. I prayed with her and stayed on the

95

phone until she had to get off. The text saying he hadn't made it came soon after we said goodbye.

Moving on can sometimes mean going back. Being there for my friend wasn't about helping her get past her grief. My part was to be there with her *during* her grief. And I was uniquely equipped. I knew there were no words, no platitudes, and not even any Bible verses that could ease the pain she felt. She needed presence—God's presence and the in-person comfort of people who loved her.

We hear a lot about the circle of life. Cue the familiar music. But in some seasons, life feels more like the circle of death—until we let God speak His message of life. God walks into grief with us. He ushers us through and reminds us that there is a new chapter about to begin. Life may not have taken the direction we expected, but God's peace is always there, and His comforting presence never leaves us behind.

A Prayer When Life Forces You Back

Those who mourn are blessed, for they will be comforted (Matthew 5:4 HCSB).

Dear Lord, I need Your help. I'm still grieving my loss, but my friend needs me. How can I help anyone? I feel inadequate for this task and for this time.

My heart is broken. Show me how I can bear another's pain. I love my friend so much, and I don't want to let her down. I needed more time before I was forced to relive this agony. Sometimes life doesn't give us the space we think we need.

Lord, You are sovereign, and You know what is best for each of us. Could it be that you are calling me here not just for her, but to help me continue to heal from my grief? Perhaps revisiting these emotions is what I need, too.

You love each of us so much. I see Your provision even in this difficult situation. Amen.

Creative Connection: Looking Back

Today, we're going to let God show us how to observe life through the rearview mirror.

Supplies
- [ ] A hand-held mirror
- [ ] This book
- [ ] Pen
- [ ] Colored pencils & other decorations for the page when you're finished.

You can do this creative connection inside or outside. I prefer to do it outside because there are more unexpected results, but it works in either place.

1. Begin by holding up your mirror and walking backwards. Use the mirror to keep from stumbling and give you a different perspective. Take your time and be safe.

2. As you walk through familiar surroundings (in your yard, around the block or in your home) notice the perspective of a unique vantage point. Notice what you see and how it looks in the rearview mirror and walking backward.

3. Ask God to apply this exercise to your circumstances right now. What insights does He give you?

4. Record what He shows you here.

5. Decorate the page.

When the Clouds Roll In

And your ears shall hear a word behind you,
saying, "This is the way, walk in it," when you turn
to the right or when you turn to the left
(Isaiah 30:21 ESV).

Navigating life after a loss seems like walking through a fog. The once familiar becomes frightening. Simple tasks turn into difficult endeavors. It's hard to get our bearings because even though there is light, it's hazy and indistinct, leaving us without a clear direction.

For all the creepiness that can accompany it, I love foggy days. Cloudy and foggy is my favorite setting for taking pictures. I know this preference seems odd—one would think I'd love sunny weather. But the beauty of a setting is often enhanced by less than perfect circumstances.

Perfect settings and ideal circumstances don't make me into the best version of myself. Easy living makes me lazy. But stormy times bring out the strength and beauty. Stress makes me rely more fully on God. Challenges force me to grow and become more Christ-like. And the struggles make me appreciate the beautiful people and circumstances surrounding me.

When I'm facing a loss—whether it's a special person or a job or opportunity—I search for the beauty in the fog. Loss makes me feel the everydayness and the take-for-grantedness more strongly. It also reframes my outlook, showing me shapes and outlines that lead me to unexpected blessings. We must learn to slow down and experience all life offers, even the foggy times. So next time the clouds roll in, look for the opportunity to experience the beauty of life in an unexpected way.

A Prayer for When the Fog Rolls In

For with You is the fountain of life; In Your light we see light (Psalm 36:9 NASB).

Dear Lord, I'm struggling to find You. I know You're there, but just like the sun on a foggy day, I can't tell where exactly You are. I want to move closer to You, but You're everywhere and nowhere.

I'm sad and nothing feels like it will ever be right again. I'm not sure I want it to be right again. It seems wrong to embrace this time of life when I'm dealing with such a devastating loss.

Help me see clearly. Guide my steps back to Your side. As I say those words, I see the lie. You *are* beside me. You *haven't* moved. All my senses are overwhelmed with the emotions of this time. Just because I don't feel the connection with You doesn't mean it's disappeared.

Clear out the fog which keeps me from feeling the comfort of Your constant presence. Put people in my life to remind me of Your constant love and attention.

Bring to my mind the Bible verses that speak Your love and care. You are my light and my guide. In You, I can have absolute faith and peace. Amen.

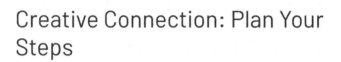

Creative Connection: Plan Your Steps

Today, we're going to take a trip—using the scenic route. Life doesn't have to go according to plan to still be packed full of God's blessings. Even when we don't know where we're going or how we're going to get there—God does. And He has already made all the plans needed.

Supplies
☐ 10 pieces of scrap paper
☐ Cup or bowl to hold the scraps while you draw them out.
☐ Pen
☐ This book

Here's what to do:
☐ Write LEFT on five of the scrap paper pieces and write RIGHT on the other five.

- [ ] Put the scraps of paper in the bowl and draw them out one at a time. Make a list of the directions in order.

- [ ] Decide whether you're going to walk or drive.

- [ ] Begin your journey and at the first intersection, follow the first direction on your list (right or left).

- [ ] Continue until you've used all the scraps of paper.

- [ ] During your journey, make note of anything interesting you observe and/or any insights God shows you regarding your grief journey and the unexpected turns you've had to make.

- [ ] Retrace your steps and finish writing about your experience.

Climbing Uphill is Hard

Now to Him who is able to protect you from
stumbling and to make you stand in the presence
of His glory, blameless sand with great joy
(Jude 1:24 HCSB).

Recovering from a loss is like climbing uphill. It takes effort and often—when we begin—it doesn't seem it will be worth the effort.

Several months ago, I joined several friends for a weekend in the mountains. The drive to the house where we were staying was tricky. It had lots of twists and turns—many unexpected. I had directions, but hadn't driven there before, so had to rely on someone else to get me where I wanted to be.

At times, the path led downhill and seemed to go places that took me away from my goal. I had to trust those who knew the path instead of relying on what I thought I saw. Because my perspective was limited and my experience with this path nonexistent. I was on the best path to reach my goal.

I couldn't see around the next turn to get my bearings. I hate traveling blind. I much prefer wide-open spaces where I can judge the path ahead and plan accordingly.

I eventually made it to the top. And the climb was well worth the effort. It wasn't just the view from the top, but the fellowship I found there as my girlfriends and I spent a wonderful weekend together.

Traveling with God is a lot like my trip to the top of the mountain. At times, it's filled with frustration as I don't appear to be going the direction I'd planned. But the process is filled with faith-stretching exercises that ultimately bring me into a closer fellowship with God. And while the climb to the top is hard, the perspective and view is always worth the faith-journey

A Prayer When the Climb is Hard

*He refreshes my soul. He guides me along the
right paths for his name's sake*
(Psalm 23:3 NIV).

Dear Lord, my path isn't one I would have chosen. I don't
have control, and I don't know for sure whether I'm
on the right track.

Life hasn't worked out the way I expected. I'm
reeling from loss and disappointment. Help me see the way
out of this valley. I want to stand on the mountaintop with
You again and know I'm where I should be and see Your
face.

You are my guide and my beacon. Help me be
attentive to Your voice during this difficult time. Teach me
to hold tight to You so I don't stumble or take a wrong turn.
Grow my faith and return my hope.

Don't let me give in to weariness and despair.
Instead, keep me tucked in close by Your side and surround

me with those who will speak Your encouragement on the hard days. Uplift my spirits and remind me that You really are still in control.

Be my road map and give me the strength to continue. You are all I need. Amen.

Creative Connection: A Time to Play

Climbing out of grief is hard work. Intense emotions take a physical toll, not to mention the mental stress of all the details to manage. So today your assignment is to take make time for play.

> Supplies
> - [ ] This book
> - [ ] Pen
> - [ ] Whatever you need to play

Your play date is to be spent with God.

In dealing with grief, many of us dread being alone. All that time to think is frightening. Today we're going to face that fear head on.

Instead of formal interaction with God, it's time to play. Do you like to be outside? Then go for a walk or a hike or a bicycle ride. If your idea of play runs more to being creative, then pull out those creative tools—paint, colored pencils, or a camera.

Keep the conversation going with God while you're playing. Talk to Him. Tell Him how you feel about your circumstances right now. Ask Him questions. Sing or listen to praise music.

At the end of your playtime, come back to this book and journal about your experience and consider making playtime with God a regular part of your routine.

Finding Beauty in Every Phase of Life

Therefore we do not lose heart. Though outwardly we are wasting away, yet inwardly we are being renewed day by day
(2 Corinthians 4:16 NIV).

Yes, I have a favorite season, most people do. Mine is autumn. I love wandering the mountains, seeing the bright sun peeking through brilliant fall leaves. To me, there's nothing as blue as a crisp October sky. I also love the blustery days this season brings, when mini tornados of leaves whirl and dance.

We can find beauty regardless of what time of year or what the weather conditions. There's wonder to be glimpsed in the dew drop poised on the edge of spring flower and joy in the first snow of winter—even beauty in the hot summer day as sunlight glints off the swimming pool. God has placed beauty around us wherever we are. We must open our eyes and see it.

I need to be reminded of this truth—especially when I'm mourning a loss. I don't want to look for beauty. But the charm and elegance of nature is there. And beauty and blessings ease me into acceptance of my circumstances.

Recognizing the good in present circumstances is critical. Watching nature in winter has helped me. If you look closely, even decaying flowers carry within them incredible beauty. And it's a beauty that is only exposed during the breaking-down process of death.

When life disassembles itself, I do my best to remember this lesson and look for the rare beauty that's only exposed during a difficult season.

A Prayer for Acceptance

*Be anxious for nothing, but in everything
by prayer and supplication with thanksgiving let
your requests be made known to God
(Philippians 4:6 NKJV).*

Dear Lord, my life has changed since my loss, and I don't like it. I want my life the way it was before. I know I'm dreaming of the impossible, but it's what I desperately desire. I don't want to become accustomed to life like this. Finding joy in my life right now seems wrong.

But I know You have allowed this for a purpose. Give me the desire to embrace my new normal. Keep me from focusing on what's gone before and allowing it to interfere with what You have planned for me now and in the future.

Give me the ability to see the beauty and blessings surrounding me. Take away the attitudes that make me unwilling to walk with You into this time. You are with me, urging me to open my eyes and experience all You have for me. Remove my rebellious spirit and replace with peace. I know You love me and have me in Your tender care. Amen.

Creative Connection: Finding Beauty Where You Are

There is beauty to find around you. Tiny steps, tiny smiles, tiny pieces of joy—all of these are important. God is the God of all creation—from majestic mountains to infinitely small strands of DNA.

Supplies
- [ ] This book
- [ ] Pen
- [ ] Colored pencils
- [ ] Ribbons and stickers to decorate this page

Go outside and sit down. You can use a chair or plop on the ground.

Now listen and look for the smallest parts of nature—animal tracks, berries on bushes, fallen leaves, insects, rocks, flowers, spiderwebs, birds, ant hills, fallen branches, weeds, worms, something round, snails, feathers.

Listen past the big and obvious and look for what's underneath. Find the beauty and the joy found in tiny.

Now record what you saw and heard. Decorate this page and ask God to give you some insight into the importance of something tiny in your own life.

Scripture Prescriptions

Prescription 1

*You will keep in perfect peace those whose minds
are steadfast, because they trust in you*
(Isaiah 26:3 NIV).

Prescription 2

*Cast your burden on the Lord, and He will sustain
you; He will never allow the righteous to be
shaken* (Psalm 55:22 HCSB).

Prescription 3

*But godliness actually is a means of great
gain when accompanied by contentment*
(1 Timothy 6:6 NASB).

Chapter Four

Welcoming Joy After Loss

Finding joy—much less welcoming—after a loss is difficult. At first, moments of joy are overshadowed with guilt. I told myself I don't deserve happiness while going through mourning. I know that's not true, but emotions are frequently deceptive. These feelings of guilt and shame are often amplified by the expectations of others—and even our own expectations.

I know the five stages of grief aren't actually a path we follow. I looked at them as a checklist and assumed once I'd dealt with one stage, I'd move on to the next. Grief doesn't work that way. A well-meaning acquaintance once told me I wasn't grieving the right way, and my personal process of mourning became a months-long journey of shame and failure.

What I believed was a series of lies. We grieve differently. As an introvert, I grieve in private. I'm not hiding my pain or purposely pushing anyone away. I'm not trying to be perceived as strong. I'm simply processing my loss in a way that is natural to how God created me. I have a friend who is an extrovert, and she needs to process grief with those she loves. This doesn't make her weak. Instead, she's learned that leaning on others *gives* her strength and it provides the blessing of allowing others the opportunity to serve.

The five phases of grief—denial, anger, bargaining, depression, and acceptance—are a list of common emotions, not stages. I experienced these stages intermittently and simultaneously—skipping one stage, like anger, and then waking up one morning immersed in rage. Knowing about these stages can be helpful because we realize what we're going through isn't unique and is a shared experience. What isn't helpful is comparing my process to anyone else's.

I've had to accept my journey of grief as my own so I can embrace joy after loss.

I need to discard any guilt I've picked up along the way. I also learned I'm not forgetting my loss by feeling joy. Joy doesn't diminish the importance of the person or circumstance that I've lost. It simply means that I'm learning to live with a precious memory. And that's good. That's what God wants me to do.

Finding Joy After The Storm of Loss

You turned my wailing into dancing; you removed
my sackcloth and clothed me with joy
(Psalm 30:11 NIV).

A river runs through our beautiful downtown Greenville, SC. I love to spend time there with my camera, especially after a big rainfall. I visited the site after a tropical storm dropped several feet of water and was astounded at what I learned.

I wandered around the park with my camera, seeing familiar landmarks in a now unfamiliar setting. The landscape was the same, yet different. A physical representation of the way life feels after devastating loss. I followed the footpaths that were open, searching for good vantage points and avoiding the mud. As I walked, my mind turned to metaphors regarding the storms of loss.

In nature, storms are necessary to clear out accumulated debris. Everywhere I turned, there were piles of unsightly trash, dislodged and now accessible for cleanup. I would never compare losing someone to taking out trash, but loss reaches deep to the buried residue inside me.

God has used the grief process to expose fragments I need to face, and now I have to do the work to change or risk covering it back up and not moving forward.

As I walked through the landscape, I was struck by the beauty that appeared in the changes. There were pools of water where once there'd been dry land and the reflections found there were new and beautiful. Losing some large trees opened up new vistas, even as I hated to see them go. Change offers unique beauty if we look for it.

Noticing all the changes also had me making a mental list of how much work there was to do to return the park to normal. It didn't take long to realize it would never be the same as it had been before. There is a new normal after a big storm. In the natural world, that means trees may have been blown down, rivers and streams have changed course, sometimes even large boulders are dislodged. Life's storms carry the same kind of changes, but we waste lots of energy trying to go back instead of moving forward.

During my time at the river, I had so much beauty to see and photograph it was almost overwhelming. If I looked up, I missed something on the ground. If I concentrated on the ground, I missed the light shimmering through winter leaves. No matter what storms of grief have raged through our lives, we still walk in beauty and joy. During times of loss, we need to give ourselves permission to slow down and see the beauty become evident.

A Prayer About Finding Joy in Changed Circumstances

Now may the God of hope fill you with all joy and peace as you believe in Him so that you may overflow with hope by the power of the Holy Spirit (Romans 15:13 HCSB).

Dear Lord, life feels offbeat. In some ways my days are filled with the familiar, but in other ways I feel like I'm wandering in an alien landscape. Help me find my bearings. I need Your foundation of love now more than ever before.

I know life doesn't stay the same, but I'm struggling to find joy in this new normal of life. By enjoying myself, it feels like I'm abandoning the person I've lost and somehow saying he was never really important. I know that's a lie, but my emotions don't seem to reflect that truth.

Show me the truth of my situation. Teach me how to remember him and also find joy. Give me the strength to move past emotions and embrace life. I'm not honoring his memory by refusing to live again.

Put people around me who don't burden me with unrealistic expectations. Use others to gently bring the lies I believe into the light where I can see them for what they are. You, oh Lord, are my truth. Lead me back to Your word and teach me to move forward in a way that brings You glory. Amen.

Creative Connection: Gratitude in the Hard Places

Even in grief, we can be grateful. Those blessings don't have to be big. But sometimes we have to be diligent to see them.

We're going to take the next seven days to practice gratitude.

Supplies
- ☐ This book
- ☐ Pen
- ☐ Colored pencils (Optional)
- ☐ Stickers (Optional)

Every evening for the next week, your assignment is to write three items or people or situations you're grateful for. I recommend the evening because gratitude for the day is a good habit to develop.

There are two rules

1. Nothing is too large or too small to go on the list.

2. Find 3 *new* items to add to your list every evening. At the end of the seven days, consider making this a regular practice.

Blooming When the Time is Right

You will make known to me the path of life;
In Your presence is fullness of joy; In Your right
hand there are pleasures forever.
(Psalm 16:11 NASB).

It was early February, and we should have had freezing temperatures, occasional flurries, and dreary days. Instead, we'd been showered with warm spring rains. The flowers were blooming and were absolutely gorgeous.

Flowers, I've noticed, don't let the calendar—or anyone's timetable—dictate their actions. They're in tune with the actual circumstances around them. When all the factors are right, they bloom.

What a powerful lesson for us as we're dealing with grief. It's so easy to use outside factors to judge our progress. We let our own expectations and those of others influence the personal timetable has for each of us.

I'm a planner and a list maker. I don't like surprises, and I'm not all that fond of drastic change. My personality is primed for judging my personal grieving process and judging myself harshly. With grief, it is impossible to follow a timetable and know what's coming next—even though I want to know.

Life rarely follows a schedule, and that's doubly true for mourning. Slowly, I'm learning to trust the circumstances around me and lean into the opportunities to bloom instead of lamenting that life isn't operating according to my original plan.

A Prayer About Thriving

*The Lord will guide you always; he will satisfy
your needs in a sun-scorched land and will
strengthen your frame. You will be like a well-
watered garden, like a spring whose waters never
fail* (Isaiah 58:11 NIV).

Dear Lord, You provide life even in the midst of death. That statement seems melodramatic since it's only my circumstances that have changed, but I'm grieving so hard right now. Nothing has gone as I expected or wanted. My dreams and expectations are in ruins around me. There's nothing left to do but pick up the broken pieces of life.

How can I thrive in these new conditions? Nothing I had hoped for is left. Where do I turn and how do I know what to do next? Can You show me how to put the pieces of my life back together?

I know nothing takes You by surprise. You promise that You have plans to bless me, but this doesn't feel like a blessing. Show me how to dig past the devastation and find the good You have for me.

Remind me of times when You've created something good from calamity. I want to exchange my sorrow for joy, but it's hard. Give me strength to focus on You and renew my hope. Use this time to grow my faith and teach me how to thrive no matter what struggle I'm facing. Amen.

Creative Connection: Plant a Seed

Healing from loss takes time. There are no shortcuts. Even though I know this, I still fight against it—especially after time has passed and I'm ready to feel better. But my emotions are still ragged and unpredictable.

Supplies
- [ ] This book
- [ ] Pen
- [ ] Packet of seeds
- [ ] Pot
- [ ] Potting soil
- [ ] Water

This exercise is one that I hope will bring you joy and insight over time. Today, I want you to plant a seed. Don't cheat by buying a small plant. Instead, get a pot, some dirt and a packet of seeds. I encourage you to choose a flower, but the choice is up to you.

After you've planted your seed, record the date, the type of seed, and how you feel about the process.

As the weeks go by, periodically record the growth of the plant.

Some suggestions:

☐ The date & feelings when you see the first green peeking through the soil.

☐ How waiting makes you feel.

☐ What God is showing you about your journey from darkness into the light.

Look Up to Find the Joy Perspective

I lift up my eyes to the hills. From where does
my help come? My help comes from the Lord,
who made heaven and earth
(Psalm 121:1-2 ESV).

Sometimes, as a photographer, I have to look up to find the best pictures. It's easy to focus on one direction and one level and miss some of the best views. The same is true in life, particularly when we've been through a season of loss.

The year 2020 was a year of loss for many of us. Some lost loved ones, some lost physical connections, and others mourned the loss of life as we'd always known it. A devastation like that can narrow a person's focus. It certainly did mine—at least for a time.

I spent hours watching the news and rehearsing everything I *couldn't* do. My thoughts swirled with the chaos surrounding me, and I felt like I was in the middle of a horrible storm. It took me a while to realize I had to change my focus, or I was going to spiral into a deep depression that would be hard to shake.

To fight that one-dimensional mindset, I changed my perspective. And I used what I'd learned through taking pictures to help. First, I slowed down. Often when I'm evaluating a setting for photography, I come to a complete stop. I look all around me. I also seek different perspectives. Sometimes this means climbing up on something or getting low to the ground. But the extra effort is *always* worth it.

I slowed down my fear-laden thoughts. I backed away from outside—panic-inducing—influences. I evaluated what was actually happening in my life. There were some major changes, but not all of them were bad. Then I physically sought a new perspective—I got on my knees and renewed my prayer life. I'd been spending so much time watching updates on the world situation, I'd let time with the Creator of that world slide into an afterthought.

When I'm taking pictures, I chase the light. I'm aware of the source of light, often moving so my subject is illuminated from behind or to one side. Or I look for a place the light is reflected. Light brings a different perspective to the scene.

I began chasing The Light—spending more time in study and reflection with God. I reorganized my day—moving things around—so that the Light became my focus. I looked for God's illumination. I also sought out people and situations where I saw His Light reflected.

Finally, I worked to be a person who clearly reflected the Light of Jesus Christ. I realized I couldn't reflect anything if my life was clouded with chaos. So, I began evaluating all the obstacles that kept me from mirroring Christ. This meant I had to clean out doubt, fear, and all the lies I had begun to accept as truth. The polishing process takes time, and it continues to this day.

All of this completely changed how I viewed my life and with that change came a return to joy. Not only did the change affect me, but it also influenced those around me.

A Prayer to Change My Perspective

Look to the Lord and his strength; seek his face
always (1 Chronicles 16:11 NIV).

Dear Lord, I know my focus is all wrong right now. I'm allowing the world to take precedence over my time with You. I can see how it's influencing my thoughts and feelings, and I don't like what's happening. But I feel powerless to stop it. I'm so sad and fearful. Everything has changed and my world is out of control.

Renew my troubled mind. Set my thoughts on You and on Your ways. Bring Bible verses to mind that remind me of all You've done. You are not a God of chaos, but of order and discipline and love. Help me remember Your love. The world would have me believe You've abandoned us, and I know that is a lie.

You are still in control, and none of these events caught You by surprise. You know the end from the beginning and yet You also know every step I take. I know You love me, and You will bring good out of it. Fill my soul with joy—Your joy—and anticipation of the wondrous ways You're working. I trust You. You are my rock and when I focus on You, the chaos becomes nothing more than a disappearing mist. Amen.

Creative Connection: A Fragrant Journey

The path through grief is full of unexpected twists and turns. That journey is punctuated by dark valleys, unexpected rays of light, and storms of emotions. And triggers come upon us when we least expect them.

Order can trigger intense memories and feelings. This creative connection is built on that fact, and it's a two-part endeavor.

Supplies
☐ This book
☐ Pen

Begin by thinking of the smells that bring back glimpses of what you've lost. Take a few minutes to write them in this section.

Now, get on your walking shoes. I want you to take a walk and let your nose lead you. If it's bad weather, go some place indoors instead. A mall is a perfect place to do this as well.

1. Once you're ready, close your eyes and take a deep breath.

2. Sort through and identify the odors. Then choose one.

3. Open your eyes and follow that smell until you reach the source, or it dissipates.

4. Now repeat the procedure.

5. Pay attention to the emotions and memories that are associated with each odor you follow.

6. Come back to this book and journal about your experience. Ask God for insight into your own grief journey.

Jagged Joy

*When I am filled with cares, Your comfort brings
me joy* (Psalm 94:19 HCSB).

In the middle of summer, I took a photography field trip
with a friend. We went early to beat the heat and hoped
to find some beautiful flowers drenched in drops of dew.
We found some of those, but it was a single jagged leaf that
caught my eye and resulted in my favorite photograph of
the day.

The edges of the leaf were brown and brittle—
missing was the smooth continuous leaf-shape that iden-
tified what tree it had fallen from. Instead, the torn edges
caught the light and created the illusion of wounds. The battle scars proved it hadn't just lightly floated to the ground,
it had been ripped from a limb and fought its way to earth.

Even in its battered condition, there in the middle
of summer, this single leaf was drenched, not in dew, but in
the vibrant reds and yellows of autumn. And although it had
lost its place in the branches, it had stayed upright between

two rocks and was positioned to catch the sun lighting it from behind. The edges were rough and almost crisp from the heat and being cut off from the tree. Still, it made me smile. The leaf's entire attitude was a kind of jagged joy—defying the season, circumstances, and loss of position.

Immediately, God nudged me toward a spiritual truth illustrated by His natural creation. No matter my circumstances, there's no excuse not to resonate with joy.

Like this leaf life leaves us with jagged edges. Circumstances do their best to tear us to pieces, but we are still here. It's important to look past the rough parts and see the colors that still shine through. Everyone part of life has something beautiful to add to our lives, and we'll find the joy if we keep our eyes open and allow God's light to illuminate it.

A Prayer to Return to Joy

*Then he said to them, "Go, eat of the fat,
drink of the sweet, and send portions to
him who has nothing prepared; for this
day is holy to our Lord. Do not be grieved,
for the joy of the Lord is your strength."*
(Nehemiah 8:10 ESV).

Dear Lord, I'm so unhappy I cannot seem to find my way back to joy. I know I've been too focused on all I've lost and ignored all the reasons to smile. Lead me back to a happier place.

You have showered me with blessings, yet I've ignored or disparaged them. Forgive me for not appreciating all You have done and are doing in my life. Change my heart so my attitude can be renewed.

Remind me that embracing joy doesn't minimize the loss I've suffered. There are those around me who say that I don't have any reason to be happy, but I know that's a lie. You've surrounded me with friends and family. I have what I need to do so much more than survive.

Don't let me sink into perpetual despair. Instead, make me an instrument of Your joy, despite of circumstances. Let others look at me and see You. I want to be an example of Your strength and resilience in the midst of struggle.

You are my strength—and more than that Your joy is my strength. Gather others around to show me all I have to be joyful about regardless of what's gone before. Amen.

Creative Connection: Learning to Be Gentle with Me

Be gentle with yourself. Grief is hard, and it can make us be hard on ourselves. We can blame ourselves or we can feel like we haven't done enough or accuse ourselves of acting or reacting incorrectly. However, you've been hard on yourself, now is the time to stop.

Supplies
- [ ] 2 smooth stones
- [ ] Paint pens or permanent markers

On the first stone, using a paint pen or a permanent ink pen, write a description of your frustration. I wrote about crying at everything. I told myself I was stupid and a baby.

Ask God to speak truth to you. Ask Him to reveal a word or a verse that releases you from that failure.

Now pick up the second rock. Write about what you learned from God.

Take the first rock somewhere and throw it away (into a lake, off a cliff, into a field).

Set the second rock somewhere in your home where you'll see it as a reminder to be gentle with yourself.

Moving Higher

He brought me out to a spacious place; He
rescued me because He delighted in me
(Psalm 18:19 HCSB).

Weariness.

Overwhelming exhaustion results from loss and is the one emotion common to almost everyone I've encountered who is grieving.

Grief inundates us with *to-dos* and *to-bes* that bury us under an avalanche of I'm-not-enough. Coping with difficult circumstances is overwhelming, no matter how strong we are.

This place called "overwhelm" leaves us tempted to hit the mental snooze and go through our days, weeks, months, and even years with eyes only half open—too tired to even try to change our attitude or seek anything different.

God was speaking to me about being overwhelmed up on the mountain that morning.

Losing my dad, even though I'd know it was coming, had left me numb. There was a service to plan, details to manage, and life to catch up on. I'd fled to God's presence in the Blue Ridge Mountains. It felt frivolous to take an entire day away, but I was desperate for renewal and rest.

It was the wisest choice I'd made in a long time.

As the car nosed the familiar way higher into the mountains, my mood rose with the elevation. Instead of being surrounded by details, I heard the whisper of God. The change in scenery helped me rise above the trivia that threatened to bury me and allowed me to once again hear from God and get His perspective on life. After that day in the mountains, I could prioritize what had to be done and weed out what didn't have to have my attention. Instead of floundering, I made real progress over the next few days.

We can get caught up in the details of life and ignore the call to get away and climb higher with God. The view where we are is nice and has some truly God moments.

But we need to keep moving higher when God calls us.

When we push through, we find a spacious place with God.

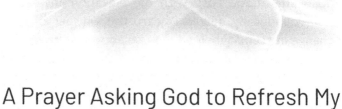

A Prayer Asking God to Refresh My Weary Spirit

And let us not grow weary of doing good, for in due season we will reap, if we do not give up (Galatians 6:9 ESV).

Dear Lord, I'm so tired. Tired of this place in my life and tired of sadness. I believe that learning to embrace joy will help revive me physically as well as mentally. Lead me into moments of joy. Open my eyes to the blessings around me.

Grant me healthy sleep, instead of nights filled with unrest. Pour Your Spirit out and refresh my soul. Help me find reasons to smile and touch my heart. Keep me from the trap of if-only.

Don't let those around me lose patience with my grieving process. Use them to help me move back into the light of living instead of the darkness of loss. I know You still have work for me, and I'm now ready to move forward on the path You've set before me.

Take away all my worrying thoughts and replace them with Your peace. You are my hope, and I want to delight again in the life You have ahead. Amen.

Creative Connection: The View From on High

When we've lost someone or something important, we can lose perspective. Grief forces us inward and down. Today we're going to physically practice a different vantage point.

Supplies
- [ ] This book
- [ ] Pen
- [ ] Colored pencils
- [ ] Tidbits to decorate this page

Drive somewhere to a high vantage point. It may mean the top of a parking garage where you can see the buildings and city below you. An alternative to driving may be walking to the top of a hill or a bluff. If you're able, you might climb a tree or go to a climbing gym and climb a wall. The point is to get up high.

Now take in the view. Spend at least twenty minutes studying the scene from this vantage point.

Record here what you see, and what God reveals to you about your changed situation.

Scripture Prescriptions

Prescription 1

*The Lord your God in your midst, The Mighty One,
will save; He will rejoice over you with
gladness, He will quiet you with His love,
He will rejoice over you with singing*
(Zephaniah 3:17 NKJV)

Prescription 2

*This is the day that the Lord has made; let us
rejoice and be glad in it* (Psalm 118:24 ESV).

Prescription 3

*Be joyful in hope, patient in affliction, faithful in
prayer* (Romans 12:12 NIV).

Chapter Five

Embracing a New Attitude

After walking through a long season of grieving, my attitude *still* needs a makeover. It's actually possible to get into a habit of sadness. You've done what they say, read all the books, tried all the tricks...but a renewed attitude still seems elusive. Joy and optimism pop up more often than they used to, but they're definitely not constant companions. What then? Are you doing something wrong? Is there something defective in your faith?

I've read about all those greats in the Bible—Joshua, Abraham, Peter, and Paul. What did they have that I don't?

Nothing.

Perspective hinders and blinds me. I know the end of their stories and that lessens the impact of their faith journey.

As I was processing where I was on the grief journey, I returned to Daniel 3:16-18—one of my favorite passages in the Bible about faith-no-matter-what.

Shadrach, Meshach and Abednego replied to him, "King Nebuchadnezzar, we do not need to defend ourselves before you in this matter. If we are thrown into the blazing furnace, the God we serve is able to deliver us from it, and he will deliver us from Your Majesty's hand. But even if he does not, we want you to know, Your Majesty, that we will not serve your gods or worship the image of gold you have set up.

I see their faith and I immediately jump to the end of the story when God did indeed rescue them—was with them in the fire. And I skip right over the fact that they felt the heat—the searing heat that killed one guard as they were forced in. And they still had to walk out an incredibly difficult path that required them to enter that furnace.

And I don't believe it was a furnace filled with joy.

Yes, there was an intense connection with God as He walked with them, a feeling of love and peace. But overwhelming joy? I doubt it.

The joy came later.

In our grief stories, we put the burden of perspective on ourselves. I don't give myself time to get out of the furnace before I demand the result.

I've learned—through experiences I wouldn't have chosen—that joy comes. But it arrives in ways we don't expect. The key to embracing a new attitude is not to squash the joy when it appears. Accept it. Enjoy it! And don't give in to the guilt that hovers in the background. Joy will come more and more often as you travel further away from the furnace and back into a new rhythm of life.

The World Isn't the Same

Every branch in me that does not bear fruit he
takes away, and every branch that does bear fruit
he prunes, that it may bear more fruit
(John 15:2 ESV)

We've lived through the pandemic. At the beginning of this insanity, we all talked about how excited we'd be when life finally returned to normal. Now the realization has sunk in that there won't be a return to that definition of normal.

Life is different, and there's no going back.

With that statement comes some hard emotions. A lot of us are mourning what we've lost. Some of the loss has been catastrophic—loved ones gone from COVID or lost in a crazy lockdown that restricted how we cared for them and ultimately mourned them. There has been lost income and lost jobs. We were denied the ability to process life together—in person—and we had to learn to interact in ways that were uncomfortable and unfamiliar. We're weary and a little shell-shocked.

How do we move on when we want so badly to return to the way things used to be? I've found that I need to accept that change—even change I didn't want or choose—isn't always bad.

One of our sons is a tree guy. He's a climber for a local company and his job is to climb to the top of the trees and either direct the cutting and pruning or do it himself. He's taught me that a lot of good comes through that kind of drastic pruning. The tree and those surrounding it are left in a healthier condition and more able to grow.

For me, 2020 was a pruning year. God cut out the deadwood and is reshaping me. I think the same can be said for our world. It's fine to mourn what we've lost, but it's equally important to continue on, learning from the hard parts and celebrating what's to come.

A Prayer When Life is Different

Have I not commanded you? Be strong and
courageous! Do not be terrified nor dismayed,
for the Lord your God is with you wherever you go
(Joshua 1:9 NASB).

Dear Lord, I don't want life to be different. I liked the way they were. I'm certain circumstances don't catch You off guard or force You to veer from Your plan. But I've been shell-shocked by the path we've been forced to take.

I feel Your presence as I walk through this change, but some days the knowledge doesn't help much. I know I need my faith and my confidence to grow, but the process is hard. Give me the resilience to keep going and stop reverting to *what-ifs*. Show me how to embrace what's ahead instead of dreading it.

I yearn for the time when life no longer feels like a contingency plan. I'm ready for my days to feel right. And yet, I resent the moments when I feel normal again. Help me reconcile all the emotions coming at me.

You promise us to never to abandon us. I've seen how You're faithful to Your word. Let me be as faithful to look to you no matter what's happening in my life. Amen.

Creative Connection: Acknowledging God's Strength Working Through You

We often sell ourselves—and God—short during difficult times. We focus so hard on the unattainable and what we think can't be done. We miss all God has already accomplished.

Today's creative connection is about noticing what God has done and what He *can* do.

> Supplies
> - ☐ This book
> - ☐ Pen
> - ☐ Colored pencils
> - ☐ Stickers and pictures to decorate this page

Begin by answering this question: What have you've been able to do during this grief journey that you didn't expect?

Write about it here. Thank God for His strength and gifting.

Now think about something you want to do. Ask God to provide the way to do that as well.

Music in the Midst of Sorrow

My lips will shout for joy when I sing praises to You; And my soul, which You have redeemed (Psalm 71:23 NASB).

I grew up in a musical house. My father was a classically trained musician and woodwinds professor at our local university. As a child, I had frequently fallen asleep listening to him practice one of the many instruments he played. Music became synonymous with love and peace.

While I have an incredible love of music, I'm not terribly proficient at it. I don't sing all that well, and I don't play an instrument. But I know a lot of technical details about music. I can read music and music has always brought me great joy.

At least it did.

Then I lost my dad in his battle with Alzheimer's. During the last few months of his life, my love of music had turned from a source of comfort to a source of pain. Listening to it—particularly to the classical music I always associated with Daddy—brought me only sorrow. After Daddy passed, I not only mourned him but also the loss of music that had once brought me joy.

Instead of a funeral the week he passed, my mother, sister and I planned a memorial service a few weeks later. Our mother was incredibly exhausted after caregiving and the act of subjecting her to an immediate funeral would have been cruel. So, we gave her—and ourselves—time to rest. My sister and I divided the planning and helped mother with every aspect of the service. I would deliver his eulogy and my sister would put together a video tribute.

It wasn't until I got into the service and heard the opening bars of Rhapsody in Blue that I realized she had used a recording of Daddy as the basis for the video. This piece of music had been dear to my dad, and he always had the clarinet solo. As grateful as I was that she had managed to get a recording of daddy playing the clarinet, I was terrified of what hearing Daddy's music could do to my composure.

But the pain I braced for never came. Instead, peace washed over me. As the music swelled and swooped, healing began. I never expected to have the joy of music return, but God gave it back to me in one thrilling instant. And with that restoration, He also gave me hope. I knew that if He could heal that part of my heart, the rest of healing would follow—in His perfect timing.

Praying for the Music to Return

I will sing to the Lord as long as I live; I will sing praise to my God while I have being (Psalm 104: 33 ESV).

Dear Lord, in my grief, my life is so silent and still. It's like being in a concert hall with no orchestra. Only memories of the joyful notes that accompanied my life remain. Part of me wants everything to stay this way. It doesn't seem right for the melody of life to continue when we've suffered such a loss.

Remind me what it was like to hear the music and feel joy. Don't let me be afraid of the memories. Keep me from worrying about moving back into the rhythm of life.

Flood my soul with Your healing symphony. While I learn to navigate this new paradigm, show me how to rest in You and find peace in Your presence.

Renew a craving for what I love to do. Don't allow them to be a source of pain but bring the joy of remembering to the forefront of my mind. You are the ultimate composer, and I know that the song of my life isn't yet finished. Give me a voice and set me back on the path walking closely with You. Amen.

Creative Connection: Write a Psalm of Praise

It seems everyone finds comfort in the Book of Psalms. I love the hopeful praise found at the end of even the most poignant psalms. Today we're going to participate in an exercise that will help us lift up our voices in praise.

Supplies
- [ ] Bible or Bible App
- [ ] This book
- [ ] Pen
- [ ] Colored pencils
- [ ] Decorations for this page

We're going to practice personalizing and paraphrasing a passage of Scripture. Praying and praising God's word back to Him is a powerful way to heal my grieving heart.

Begin by asking God to give insight and peace.

Next, choose a Psalm—one of your favorites or one of those listed below:

- ☐ Psalm 11
- ☐ Psalm 28
- ☐ Psalm 63
- ☐ Psalm 146

Write it here and personalize it as you go. Add your name instead of pronouns. Be specific about your current struggles and mindset.

Encouragement Now

*So we don't look at the troubles we can see now;
rather, we fix our gaze on things that cannot
be seen. For the things we see now will soon
be gone, but the things we cannot see will last
forever* (2 Corinthians 4:18 NLT).

I've mentioned before that fall is my favorite time of year. I love the crisp days, the beautiful leaves and all the scents that come with the season. By the time August rolls around, I'm sick of the heat and begin anticipating autumn. And sometimes I find a preview of what's ahead. A promise that no matter how hot and miserable I am right now, fall will come again.

Late summer days that begin with an unexpectedly cool—humidity free—morning. Or I catch a whiff of pumpkin-spice. Hints that this season won't last forever. My favorite previews are found in nature. I love spotting—prematurely—brilliant fall leaves framed by a canopy of greenery.

God gives us previews of life too. Several times He's given me a picture of something new that's coming in my life and then—when I least expect it—He shares a preview of the anticipated new normal. Encouragement comes in a positive word from someone or a small success that renews my hope. I don't even have to be paying close attention. In a hot, weary season, God drops something beautiful right in the middle of normal life.

When I glimpse autumn-colored leaves against summer, it's a reminder that God loves me enough to put encouragement in my path. He never forgets me or loses track of where I am or when I need a sign that a refreshing season is just around the corner.

A Prayer for What's to Come

Many are the plans in the mind of a man, but it is
the purpose of the Lord that will stand
(Proverbs 19:21 ESV)

Dear Lord, I know that You have only the best planned for me. But right now, I can't see past my current circumstances. How can I find good in such tragedy, and how can You want me to find good in what I'm facing today?

I trust You, though. Bring to my mind all the ways You've brought blessings from bad times. Don't let me become consumed with the stress and sorrow around me. Keep my mind set firmly on You.

Surround me with people who will speak Your goodness and blessings to me. I need the influence of Your people right now. Give me support as I walk through this time.

Put previews of joy in my path today. Punctuate my day with moments of hope. Replace my sadness with anticipation. Change the attitude of my heart from mourning to contentment. I can't imagine how You'll affect that change, but I know You can. More than that, I have faith that You will. You are my hope and in You I place all my trust. Amen.

Creative Connection: Say Yes to Life

It's hard to relearn the habit of moving forward after a devastating loss. This creative connection helps get you started. The supplies for this one are basic.

　　Supplies
　　　　☐　This book
　　　　☐　Pen
　　　　☐　Colored pencils
　　　　☐　Trinkets and flourishes to decorate this page

　　Begin by listing ten positive activities you'd like to do over the next six months. Now choose one of them and ask God to help you begin that one thing today!

My Top 10 List for the Year

1.

2.

3.

4.

5.

6.

7.

8.

9.

10.

    Come back to this list periodically and choose another item. Continue until they're all accomplished.

Perfectly Imperfect

*But He said to me, "My grace is sufficient
for you, for power is perfected in weakness."
Therefore, I will most gladly boast all the
more about my weaknesses, so that
Christ's power may reside in me
(2 Corinthians 12:9 HCSB).*

I love flowers. I love taking pictures of flowers—especially close-up shots. Choosing blossoms as the focus of my pictures has allowed me to study the details found in these beautiful blooms. And I've discovered some timeless truths during the process.

There's no such thing as a perfect flower. I should know, I've searched high and low for one. They look amazing from a distance, but when I come in for a closer inspection, I always find flaws.

Life is like that. From a distance, others' lives may seem perfect. But if we take the time to look closer, we'll see the fragility. If I'm truthful, much of my dissatisfaction with life stems from comparison. Studying nature has made me realize I can't accept what I see from a distance as the full and accurate picture.

The flaws don't detract from the overall beauty of the flower. Not being perfect doesn't interfere with my enjoyment of a blossom. Neither does its lack of perfection detract from a flower's fulfillment of its purpose.

Because my life isn't perfect—or the way I want it to be—doesn't mean it isn't meaningful. God has a purpose for my life. He has a long-term purpose and a purpose right now, in all that I'm facing. It's so easy to gauge my usefulness by whether everything is going the way I think it should.

Many times, I obsess over performing with excellence and then feeling like a failure when I'm less than perfect. That's especially true when I'm in a crisis or experiencing a loss. I'm trying to live up to my expectations and the perceived expectations of those around me. Instead, God wants me to rest. He's allowed this season for a purpose, and it's time to quit being so hard on myself.

A Prayer for Peace Instead of Perfection

To shine upon those who sit in darkness and the
shadow of death, To guide our feet into
the way of peace (Luke 1:79 NASB).

Dear Lord, I want to pass through this season well. I don't want to disappoint You or anyone that's around me. But I'm so weary of striving for perfection. All I want to do is hide in my room and cry my eyes out.

Yet who am I to know what should be?

Life isn't the way I want it to be. I don't want to move forward into this new paradigm. I have no choice. There's no going back, I know that. I'm trying to move forward in a way that honors You.

And that's where the wheels come off. In my striving to be the best, I'm just tired. My emotions are a mess of confusion. They attack me without warning and leave me gasping with their intensity. I swing between wanting to accept my life and wanted to throw a tantrum. Sometimes I don't know what I'm truly feeling.

Clear out the chaos. Replace my urge to work well with Your rest. Show me how to walk through this time with You and leave my expectations behind. Remind me You love me no matter what I'm feeling. Give me the courage to lean into You without judging myself. Amen.

Creative Connection: Words of Peace and Hope

When we're grieving, hope and peace can be in short supply. With this creative connection, we're going to let God give us a ready supply of hope.

Supplies
- ☐ Small envelope or bag
- ☐ Sheet of paper
- ☐ Pen
- ☐ Colored Pencils
- ☐ Stickers and scraps to decorate your envelope
- ☐ Tape or glue

Crumple a sheet of paper. This represents life right now—messy and imperfect.

Cut the paper into pieces that are big enough to write a word or two on. They can be symmetrical or random sizes—your choice.

Ask God to give you words and Bible verse references that will encourage you now and in the days to come.

Write one word or Bible verse reference on each piece of paper.

Put the scraps of paper in your envelope or container.

Decorate the envelope or container.

Keep it in a prominent place, so it's always there when you need it. I taped mine here in this book, so I always know where it is. Pull the words out as needed.

Subtle Changes

The steadfast love of the Lord never ceases;
his mercies never come to an end; they are
new every morning; great is your faithfulness
(Lamentations 3:22-23 ESV).

We took a trip and stayed in a hotel overlooking the Ohio River. Of course, I couldn't resist the sunrise views.

This first morning, I practically ran to the water's edge because of the intensity of color. At first, it was an incredible orange-red. The sky was so vibrant, it almost looked angry. The fire-like quality of the color was at complete odds with the freezing temperature. I'd never experienced a sunrise like that before.

I continued to snap pictures as I recorded the subtle changes in the scene. The sky softened, and the colors muted, and the freezing temperature receded. The sun rose over the horizon. The intensity faded, and the world warmed as it returned to normal.

It was an incredible experience.

My mind settled on grief because of what we've experienced in the past year.

At first, our lives were flooded with that dark, violent color of loss. It froze our hearts and minds and was like nothing I'd ever experienced. Our entire world was changed in an instant.

But then, almost imperceptibly, the intensity receded. As time passed, the more familiar colors of life returned. For me, it was drawing closer to God and allowing Him to once again flood my life with the warmth of His love. He has introduced us to a new rhythm for life—not one we'd have ever chosen—but still filled with beauty and a little more joy every day.

A Prayer About Subtle Changes

Cast all your anxiety on him because he cares for you (1 Peter 5:7 NIV).

Dear Lord, You know how much I hate change. Yet it's what I'm begging for. I'm so weary of being sad. I don't want to forget, but I desperately want to feel something more than grief.

I'm exhausted by the emotions that rampage in my heart and mind. I need Your peace. Lead me out of this valley and back into the constant place of well-being.

Show me how to feel joy without guilt. Thaw out the ice that's encased my heart and let me feel again. I'm afraid to open myself up too much because the pain of loss may once again overwhelm me.

Restore my balance. Set my feet on a firm foundation. Bring to mind the joy of before the tragedy and provide opportunities for me to do them again. Surround me with caring friends who will help ease me back into life's daily routine.

Ease my anxiety when dark thoughts threaten. Remind me of the good times so I can remember without the intense pain. I never want to forget, but I want to leave the pain behind.

You are my rock and my salvation. Your presence has held me in the darkest hours. I know that dawn has come, You are still with me and will never abandon me. Amen.

Creative Connection: Haiku

There is healing in creating a haiku. Don't dodge this simple exercise.

Supplies
- ☐ This book
- ☐ Pen
- ☐ Colored pencils
- ☐ Decorations

Consider your grief journey and how God *has* been present with you through this difficult time. On the next page, write words showing the pain and the peace of God. Here is the poetic form for writing a Haiku.

- ☐ Line one – 5 syllables
- ☐ Line two – 7 syllables
- ☐ Line three – 5 syllables

Now decorate this page with your Haiku in the middle.

Haiku

Scripture Prescriptions

Prescription 1

> *Trust in the Lord with all your heart And*
> *do not lean on your own understanding.*
> *In all your ways acknowledge Him, And*
> *He will make your paths straight*
> (Proverbs 3:5-6 NASB)

Prescription 2

> *May the words of my mouth and the meditation*
> *of my heart Be acceptable in Your sight, Lord, my*
> *rock and my Redeemer* (Psalm 19:14 NASB).

Prescription 3

> *But thanks be to God, who gives us the victory*
> *through our Lord Jesus Christ*
> (1 Corinthians 15:57 ESV).

About Edie Melson

Find your voice, live your story... is the foundation of Edie Melson's message, no matter if she's reaching readers, parents, military families, or writers. As an author, blogger, and speaker she's encouraged and challenged audiences across the country and around the world. Her numerous books reflect her passion to help others develop the strength of their God-given gifts and apply them to their lives.

In addition to being a writer, Edie has this to say, "I'm creative out of self-defense. As the daughter of an artist-mother and musician-turned-photographer-father, I'd have been a disgrace if I hadn't been true to my creativity." Edie also dabbles in photography, bullet journaling, and knitting.

Edie's a popular speaker and a board member of the Advanced Writers and Speakers Association. You can find her blogging regularly on www.Soulfulink.com, www.AriseDaily.com, and Just18Summers.com. Connect with her on her website, www.EdieMelson.com and through Instagram, Twitter, and Facebook.

Made in United States
Orlando, FL
30 November 2021

10948438R00104